On Contemporary Seidr: A Guide to Norse Trance Work

KURT HOOGSTRAAT

Copyright © 2019 Kurt Hoogstraat

All rights reserved.

ISBN: 9781072711896

Dedication:

to Ivy Mulligan for being eternally optimistic

to Stephan Gunn for his input and masterful editing skills

to Matthew Sargent, Saga Erickson, and Todd Spencer for keeping me on track

to Stephan Grundy for support in every aspect of the creation of this book

to my apprentices for constantly pushing me forward

and most importantly, to my amazing husband Jon without whom not a word would have been written

Introduction

This isn't your Great Aunt Betsy's seidr!

This is a book about Contemporary Seidr. I call what I do and teach Contemporary Seidr because it is not the kind of traditionally-known Seidr. It's not exactly the kind of Seidr found mentioned ever-so-briefly in the Norse lore, but a type of Seidr that is influenced by other different practices and traditions. It is a style of Seidr that is closely akin to Shamanic practices found in other cultures and traditions.

Traditional Seidr is the kind of work that involves the seer to sit in a high seat and be sung by a chorus into trance. Contemporary Seidr is much less complex. Contemporary Seidr is what I personally practice and teach to my apprentices and will be talking about in this book. I will use the phrase Contemporary Seidr to help delineate between these two different types of trance work. Another phrase that covers my type of work is "soul work." So, whenever I say Contemporary Seidr if you'd rather just substitute the phrase "soul work." What it's called is less important than the actual process described herein.

Just as other Proto-European cultures had their Shamans, the Norse culture certainly had their own practicing this type of work. The Norse culture was a rich and vibrant example of the other cultures of their times. Whether Bronze Age or Stone Age, whichever Age you choose to explore, the Norse were there keeping up with their neighbors. Theirs was a diverse culture encompassing law, medicine, and the arts. Why then would they not have their spiritual leaders? These were the Shamans. The Vitkis and Volvas.

A Vitki is a Norse Shaman. They perform many of the same tasks assigned to the Shamans of different cultures. Trance work to go to other Realms to retrieve information. Healing. Divination. A Volva is the female counterpart to the Vitki. These of course are very loose and broad definitions. But they are definitions based on current understanding of the roles played by very special folks in ancient times. In this book I will concern myself with just one aspects of their functions. This is Norse trance work.

The workers of Seidr are, at their core, Norse Shamans. To embrace this fact freely opens the multiverse of the current day worker of Contemporary Seidr in ways I can't even begin to describe. Vitkis and Volvas, or Norse Shamans, are of the tradition we follow.

So many of our practices are similar or even identical to the Shamans of other cultures. Journeying and the use of drums are just two examples of how our work is identical to the work of Shamans throughout the world. Our ancestral spiritual leaders were well versed in augury, the divination or the reading of signs of other sorts such as the Runes and much more. The act of journeying to gain wisdom and answers to life's most difficult questions would certainly have fallen upon the Shamans. Call him the Vitki. Call her the Volva. They were the Shamans of their tribes.

The Vitki lived at the fringes of the societal system known as the tribe. Valued members of the tribe yes. But apart. This separateness was needed to do their job the most effectively. They needed space and free rein to experience nature and all its glory. They needed to be a part of the natural world even more than they needed to be part of the tribe. Hence the separation from society as they knew it.

It is not my aim with Contemporary Seidr to throw out all the wisdom that comes from the traditions of our ancestors. Rather Contemporary Seidr is all about using traditional practices as a foundation for Seidr work. There is such a rich history from our past that simply cannot be denied. Contemporary Seidr seeks to build upon the ways of the past.

Several books have been written about traditional Seidr and its history. I list some of them at the back of this book. Also, a quick Google search can yield more information on this subject. It is the hope that this book will shed light on a new tradition of Seidr that is growing rapidly. This new tradition is labeled Contemporary Seidr.

What is Contemporary Seidr? It is a method of trance work that can be done alone or for small groups. It doesn't require a chorus of singers to sing you off to the Nine Realms. Or a Volva in her high seat. It does entail the traveling of the Nine Realms to seek wisdom and guidance. Traveling to Hel to speak with departed ones. Many of the skills assigned to traditional Seidr workers. But in a much more personal and hopefully reachable type of trance work.

So, what makes this Seidr and not simply another more generic form of trance work? Well it relies heavily on the Norse pantheon and Nine Realms. It is set in the cosmology of the Norse world. As trance work it is definitely similar to other traditions. It may fly in the larger more universal cosmos, but it has its feet planted firmly in the world of the Northern traditions.

I am no guru. I don't have all the answers. So many questions are yet to be asked how could I already have all the answers? This book like any book is based on personal experiences. As such it is opinion. But I will say I know what I know. And that's what I share here.

There is really no big mystery surrounding this method. It is grounded and rather common. It is about trance which may sound intimidating, but I believe that anyone who puts in the time can accomplish results. You can do any of the exercises here and benefit from them. It all depends on your ability to dedicate yourself to this practice. Results will probably not come immediately but I believe they will come although as with all Esoteric work results cannot be guaranteed. Perseverance is one of the main keys to success in this work. As my father called it "sticktoitiveness". Simple as that.

This book hopes to be highly personal. Seidr is a spiritual activity and spiritual practices cannot help but be personal. I will share with you what I have learned through years of experimentation and now use in a settled practice. I am a full time Vitki. What you'll discover in this book is part of what I teach to my apprentices. So, what I offer is merely personal opinion based on experience. I don't claim to be an expert at anything. But I do know these methods work effectively for me and others I have met on my path.

It is my goal to guide you to aspects of the multiverse that our ordinary eyes don't see. Let this book serve as a travel guide. Take the chance to go along with me on this amazing and life-changing journey. Take your first steps now.

Disclaimer

This book in part deals with matters pertaining to the psyche. Some exercises given are meant to address such issues. But by no means are they meant to be a substitute for psychiatric or psychotherapeutic care. If you are under the care of mental health professionals check with them before doing these exercises.

A bit about me

Who is this guy? Where did he come from? What gives him the right to write a book on Contemporary Seidr anyway?

Good questions. I ask myself these things all the time. Here is the way I answer myself.

I first started calling myself a Vitki over 25 years ago. That's when I first joined the Rune Gild. I came across the title Vitki during my studies with them. According to the Rune Gild and the books of its founder Edred Thorsson anyone who studies the Runes is a Vitki. Well that was me! So, I had a label to give myself.

Years of studying went by. I ultimately branched out into studying Seidr about 15 years ago when I felt my practice had become unbalanced. I was much too focused on the masculine side of esoteric things that I needed a little feminine energy. That's why I turned to Seidr. Freyja taught it to Odin. So why not me? Of course, I read every book I could find on Seidr and trance in general. More studying and learning.

About 5 years ago I felt confident enough in what I knew that I asked the multiverse and the gods for apprentices. And they came to me. Thank the gods because I have learned and experienced so much through working with them.

I decided to start a Facebook group devoted to the work of Vitkis and Volvas. And people joined! I was amazed that so many people were following this path. But they were and are! A wonderfully vivid community of people who dedicate themselves to the esoteric path of the Norse ways.

I studied with Vitkis from both Kiev and England. Both offered me much wisdom and knowledge. I wouldn't be who I am today if I hadn't spent time with these two remarkable men.

I received my certification as a core Shaman. This was big for me because I had been doing this work for years and it was fulfilling to have an organization recognize me. It's a certificate I have proudly hanging on my ritual room wall.

All these years I have never stopped learning and growing on this path. I have been doing this work full time for the past eight years. I do what a Shaman does every day. I walk this path in all my daily affairs. It has been so for many years.

So that in a nutshell is who I am. This is what I bring to the table. I am largely spirit lead. But spirit has led me far indeed. This is what I offer you in this book. It is a humble way for me to give back as thanks for all I've received. May you as well find yourself being spirit lead. It is a journey well worth taking.

About this book

Here's a little bit about this book and what to expect. And what not to expect. Do not turn to this book looking for the words of a guru. I am not that. What I am is a certified core Shaman of the Norse path who in many ways has been spirit taught. I have been practicing this path for quite a while. And what this book offers you is a glimpse into my workings and the workings I teach my apprentices. I have had great success and grand failure in my years of trial and error. I hope to offer what I've learned along my journey on this path.

Put this book down. Often. It is meant to be experienced. Not read all the way through. Only by doing the exercises outlined and thinking about the things I bring up in the text will you get the full benefit of this book. May as well get what you paid for!

This book is not the only way to approach Contemporary Seidr work. It's merely a retelling of what works for me and my many apprentices over the years. There is no right or wrong way to approach this. What follows is what works for me. My hope is that it will provide you a structure or skeleton to build upon.

This book is not meant to contain an ending. Merely openings to your own studies. Take what I say in these pages as a jumping off place for your own personal practice. If you do just that this book will have served its purpose. I could hope for nothing greater.

So, sit back. Get comfy. And let the ride begin...

Tools

This is a list of tools that you may find helpful in your Contemporary Seidr work. None of them are absolute necessities, but they are the tools that I find helpful in my work. One of the biggest things about approaching Contemporary Seidr work is a willingness to experiment. Try things out. See what does or doesn't work for you. So have fun experimenting with these items. See what works for you!

1. Comfortable chair. This is the only item that is absolutely needed. You will be spending a lot of time in this chair for sessions that can last up to 30 minutes. You don't want to be interrupted by having to shift about to get comfortable. The chair should have a back on it to help you stay steady through sessions that may include swaying. Everything that makes it easier to shift consciousness should be considered in choosing a chair. And the placement of the chair is important. It should be in a room or area of your house where you will not be disturbed. You need to be able to spend uninterrupted time there. A comfy seat is needed in an undisturbed place. So there. I guess there's one thing on the list that I deem a necessity. Although now that I think of it, I do have a star apprentice who finds it easiest to sit on the ground for his Contemporary Seidr work!

You may also want to invest in a high seat. This is a taller than average chair or seat. In traditional Seidr work the Volva serving as the Oracle would be seated on a high seat. I do have one for work with clients. Elevating myself adds to the overall impression of dignity to the proceedings when others are present. But in all honesty my high seat is really a padded swiveling bar stool bought at Walmart. Hey! It works is all!

2. Journal or notebook. You're going to want to keep track of your experiences in the other Realms. A journal will assist you in that goal. It also serves as a handy tool to help track your progress.

3. Drum or drum track. This is to assist you in getting into trance. The rhythmic beat of a drum may be monotonous, but it serves as the perfect sound to get you to an altered state of mind. Focusing your attention on the beat also helps give your mind something to do. If you don't want to invest in an actual drum you may want to use a prerecorded drum track for the same results. Either way, it's an excellent way to get into and altered state of consciousness.

If you make the decision to invest in a drum, which I would encourage you to do, they can be purchased in many sizes and hides from talented crafts folk. I have several small drums 10 inches across and one larger one of 18 inches across. I use them all depending on my needs for the Contemporary Seidr work at hand.

Smaller drums have a higher tonal quality than larger drums. These are excellent for drumming your way to Asgard or any of the Upper Realms. Larger drums with a deeper tone are great for journeys to Hel. I like being able to suit my drum to my purpose. But for years I only had a smaller drum. It worked fine for me. I was just finally able to financially afford some more choices.

All my drums are made from natural hides. I have an elk and several horse hide drums. If it's possible a natural hide is preferable. It keeps us closer to the traditions of our ancestors. But if you have animal allergies or simply can't afford a natural hide drum, having a drum with a synthetic head is definitely great. As long as it can keep a beat! Rattles are also used to journey effectively.

I have several decorated drums and several plain ones. The decorated ones have graphics painted on the top of the heads. One of my small drums (okay my favorite) has the Elder Futhark of Runes painted on it! But decorated or not is really just a matter of personal taste.

I first came across the use of drums to enter an altered state back in the early 1980s when I attended a drumming circle with a friend. As the group sat there and drummed even, I was entered into a type of trance. When I started pursuing this path seriously, I made sure to get a drum!

Handcrafted drums and rattles can easily be purchased through Etsy or even Amazon. Try Etsy for the fact that the drums offered there tend to be made by people on spiritual paths like those we are on. I know Gaia's Workshop Drums is staffed by heathens and they make excellent drums!

The pounding of a drum also acts as a repetitive motion which definitely assists in getting into trance. Just like the act of swaying gently back and forth can help you achieve a trance the action of pounding a drum can be used as a great aide.

Drum tracks are available on CD or digitally through places like iTunes. Look for recorded tracks for Shamanic purposes. Many exist and should be easy to find.

4. Staff. A traditional Vitki/Volva tool but one that still works. Get a staff to hold on to in order to help keep yourself grounded in Contemporary Seidr sessions. Or use it in place of a drum to beat out a rhythm by pounding it on the floor. Decorate it with small bells for added rhythm making sounds. For a detailed description of an outfit worn by a Volva documented in the lore check out "The Saga of Erik the Red."

Staffs like drums can be found on Etsy. I got my staff from Amazon for a very reasonable price! But it's beautiful and does a great job. You can also craft your own staff from a downed branch of a tree. Just make sure it's finished enough that there are no splinters.

Staffs can be as simple or ornate as you desire. For the best results try to get one at least 4 feet tall. You want to be able to use it to help you walk over outdoor terrain if you plan on doing any journey work in nature.

5. Cloak. Use a hooded cloak. Get one with a hood big enough to pull up over your eyes and block your vision. The point of this is to induce darkness so you'll be less distracted. Beautiful cloaks are readily available through many sources. Just be sure to choose one where the hood is big enough to pull over your head and cover your eyes.

Cloaks are part of more traditional garb. But they can definitely be effective in Contemporary Seidr as well. Whether you choose a simple rough linen or velvet try to make sure its dark in color. The point beyond decorative is to block out the light.

6. Incense or scented oils. Scent is a powerful trigger. Pick a scent that you will only use in Contemporary Seidr sessions. This will serve as a trigger for your brain that you're about to go into a working trance. Pick an earthy deep scent like patchouli or lavender. Nothing too stimulating like the citruses. You want it to be conducive to remaining relaxed and open.

Scented oils can also prove useful. Dab a bit just under your nose to get the full effect.

A scent that is common to use on the Norse path is mugwort. This is the scent that I use for my work. It is earthy and grounding. It's important to think about keeping yourself grounded while doing this work. I recommend doing a grounding ritual before each session. Remember we want to keep one foot firmly planted in ordinary consciousness. A quick grounding ritual helps to do this.

7. Music. Music also serves as a powerful trigger. Pick something with a lot of drums and some chanting. Maybe pick out something where the chants are in a foreign language, so you won't be distracted by listening along to lyrics. Check out the bands Danheim or Wardruna. Both are types of music that I use and highly recommend. Both are heavy on rhythm and chant in languages that don't distract me. Have some fun researching and picking out music to use!

That's a quick list of tools you might find helpful on this journey. Again experiment. Find out what works for you and use it! Just remember that tools are there to be used as aides in your journeying. They should never serve as a focus of your work. But they can be powerful allies. So, try some on for size. And finding just the right tool can be a powerful experience in itself. Happy exploration!

What kind of trance anyway?

When I talk about and teach trance what exactly do I mean? That you're going to be unconscious and unresponsive to the world as we know it? Absolutely not. That kind of deep trance is not what we're going for in Contemporary Seidr as I teach it. The kind of trance I mean is what I call a working trance. This is when you have one foot firmly rooted in ordinary consciousness and the other foot in another of the Nine Realms. But is this even possible? Yes. Think of it as something akin to the type of consciousness you have when you're about to fall asleep or not quite fully awake in the morning. You can hear things and see things, but your consciousness is altered somewhat. There's an altered state of awareness. That's the kind of trance I'm after. That way you can do sessions alone and still reap the benefits of trance. You'll be able to recall all you've seen and heard without the fear of forgetting it. This in my experience is the most powerful form of trance. You are still in control but relaxed enough to truly receive messages from the other Realms.

The challenge of going "totally under" is that unless someone else is there for you to communicate your impressions to firsthand you are apt to forget these impressions entirely when you fully return to ordinary consciousness. By keeping one foot in the ordinary consciousness you can jot things down in a journal. A journal is an important tool to have as it gives you the opportunity to recount your visions. It also serves as a way to track your progress on this path. It will do your heart good after six months' worth of practice to go back to your earliest entries and see just how much you've grown!

Getting to this state of working trance is not terribly difficult. With some perseverance I believe almost anyone can achieve this level of trance. But you have to be ready to give it the old college try. There are several methods to get into this kind of trance. I will outline some a little later on. But I assure you there is more than one way to skin a cat!

So, this all is what I mean when I say "trance." A working trance in which you'll still have control over your body and yet be open to the messages from the multiverse. It's a perfectly natural state of mind. Nothing spooky or odd about it at all. So have no fear!
 I'll be taking you down a path you've already traveled before. As we travel you may have a distinct sense of deja vú. You have seen this all before. You have just forgotten it for now. As for my role in this journey I'm just your tour guide!

Getting started

Okay now. Where do we begin the journey? With first steps of course! And in Contemporary Seidr, the first step is getting to be able to have a shift in your consciousness. That all begins with meditation.

I hear the naysayers already. "I've tried to meditate. But I just can't." "My mind is never quiet enough to meditate." "What kind of nonsense is he talking about anyway?"

Well I assume that if you're reading this book you have more than a passing interest is getting into trance. Contemporary Seidr is at its heart a form of trance work after all. Trance work means altered states of consciousness. And meditation is where it all begins.

Here's how I do it. Sit in your comfy chair and maybe light a candle or grab a crystal to use as a focal point. Try playing some soft volume music. Have some incense burning. Anything to help you relax. It's all about achieving a relaxed state of body where your mind relaxes too. Keep your vision blurry. Ignore background noises to the best of your abilities. Count down backwards from ten.

Now breathe. Breathe with intention. In four counts hold four counts and out four counts. If you can't do it to the count of four try three. The point is to establish a rhythm. Do this until you don't need to count anymore, and the rhythm is established. Keep breathing in this rhythm for a while until it feels natural and comfortable.

Now focus on your focal object. The candle flame. The crystal. And try not to think! Just kidding. The brain thinks. That's what it's built to do. So, you will have thoughts. Sometimes slowly appearing and at other times coming as rapidly as water gushing from a faucet. Thinking is just a byproduct of being alive. What to do?

Just acknowledge the thought. Admit that it's there. But don't give it any more power than that. Acknowledge the thought and tell it that you're doing something else very important right now. And assure the intruding thought that you'll get back to it later. Push the thought away gently. And sure enough your mind will be clear. It's as easy as that. For now. But the thoughts will return. And just repeat the process of letting go. A technique one of my apprentices uses is to in his mind's eye walk away from the thoughts. He has an image of the thought being there as physical entities and just walks away. That works wonders for him.

Soon enough you'll find the thoughts will stop coming as rapidly and slow down to a mere trickle. It's now that you can start looking for that shift in consciousness.

You may experience this shift as a gentle almost falling asleep feeling. Or it may come suddenly and profoundly. I experience it as a heightened sense of my awareness through the five typical senses. Be open to whatever kind of shift you may experience. Rest assured you will know when the shift occurs. You will be experiencing a state of mind unlike your ordinary consciousness. It will feel...different is all I can say. But once you've experienced it, you'll know.

A bit about grounding and centering. These are important skills to get under your belt at this early stage. Without grounding who knows where you'll end up? Maybe someplace not very nice.

To ground is very easy. Sit with your feet flat on the ground. As you get into your rhythmic breathing on the inhale imagine you're pulling energy up from the ground. Imagine this energy flowing up your feet and legs. Soon it fills your torso and your head. That's what you want. To be filled with the energy from the ground. This keeps you centered and able to energetically do your session.

On the exhale imagine roots from the bottom of your feet pushing deep into the ground. Deeper and deeper the roots grow. Solidly planting you in the ground. That's what I mean by grounding.

And that's the key to a working trance. The first step. Congrats! You're on your way!

More ways

Remember that a large part of this work is experimentation. Here are some other ways to try achieving the shift in consciousness.

Try repetitive motion. This sort of activity lulls your mind into a kind of inaction that leaves it possible for messages to get through. In this receptive state you will be able to react to the multiverse in profound ways. A couple of types of repetitive motion work well. Swaying back and forth in a rhythm works well for some people. This simple yet effective method is a mainstay for me in my practices. For more detailed information on this technique please check out the book "Seidways", by Jan Fries. Other folk pound a drum. I do this along with the swaying for a double whammy effect. But don't think it's limited to those two. Any kind of motion you can sustain long enough to feel the shift in consciousness will do the trick. Remember not to give up. Keep trying until you've achieved your goal. Or your muscles give out!

Try the scent. Either incense or a scented oil can help train your brain to the fact that something different is about to happen. Use the scent along with another method of achieving the shift. The trigger of scent will with practice become so strong that just smelling the scent will help to induce the working trance. Shortcuts like this aren't cheating. They're using your tools in appropriate ways to achieve trance.

Chant or sing. Chanting something like the Runes in a form of galdr works wonders. I often chant the name of the deity I'm trying to get in contact with or the name of the Realm I'd like to travel to. Or make up a simple repetitive song to quietly sing to yourself. In traditional Seidr helpers sing the Oracle to the other Realms. This is documented in the lore. And so, in Contemporary Seidr it can be a powerful tool for yourself to use solo.

Another method is the guided meditation. In this method you imagine yourself on a grassy field. Looming in front of you some distance away is Yggdrasil. You walk towards the tree. As you get closer you notice how huge and big around it is. At last you're there. You see a door in the massive trunk. You open the door. The inside of the tree is hollowed out. An eerie otherworldly light illuminates it. You notice a spiral staircase in the center of the hollow. It goes both up and down. Depending on where you wish to travel you start going up or down the stairs. With each step you feel yourself relaxing. The stairs lead to landings with doors opening out. Beyond those doors are the separate Realms. This method is especially good for those who just don't feel the shift using any other method.

Try as many methods as you can. Try it sitting up or laying down. Try it with a drum or drum track. Try singing. Try them all! All are valid ways to achieve the shift in consciousness. And as many ways as you can have success with, the more tools you'll have in your Contemporary Seidr toolbox. That's the goal. In case one day one method doesn't work you'll have options to fall back on. That's real power.

What to expect

How do I know if I've arrived at an altered state? How do I know this shift of consciousness has occurred? Good question. Here's some ways of knowing if you've arrived.

Close your eyes. Remain open to any images you may receive. They may come in the form of movies in your mind. They may appear as simply color blocks. You may get auditory impressions or messages. The key is to remain open to however the multiverse tries to communicate with you. It's not so hard to receive these messages. We receive them all the time. We just haven't paid attention to them. We write them off as daydreams or random thoughts. I get them as messages from the other Realms and treat them as such.

To know the difference between authentic messages and just simply totally random thoughts and daydreaming ask a few key questions. Is what I'm receiving in 3D and technicolor? Is there a truly heightened sense of reality to what I'm getting? Does it feel unlike my ordinary consciousness in ways that are obvious to me? Is it somehow hyper real? Those are all ways to know if the shift has occurred and you're now dealing with a working trance.

Again, you will not be totally under and unaware of what's happening. You'll be able to be aware of important things happening in your ordinary consciousness, like someone entering your room or speaking to you. Changes in light will be noticed. This is one of the reasons to do this work with just a candle or the hood of a cloak over your eyes. Or even a towel over your head! Anything to cut down on the distractions. You will hear the doorbell ring. Children playing outside. Which could be a reason to invest in a white noise machine or use music. You will be faintly aware of such things. But you will also be aware of a new heightened state of awareness. This is the world of the working trance.

You may also feel a sense of tingling or vibration to your physical self. That's normal. You're getting energies you're not used to having that now impact your awareness. Go with that feeling. Remain open. Let yourself see where these new sensations may take you. It's all about being open to the multiverse and experimenting. Let yourself go.

Hopefully this helps you better understand what it is we're looking for. If you're experiencing this new heightened sense of reality and getting images that are not of your own active mind's creation, congratulations! You're in a working trance! Now comes the fun stuff...

Hold on

Now you've experienced the shift in your consciousness to the working trance state. Maybe just for a second. Maybe a whole minute. But that's not long enough to have an actual Contemporary Seidr session. Contemporary Seidr sessions can last up to 30 minutes. How to hold on to that state for that long?

A large part of it has to do with intention. I'll talk about intention in this book quite a bit. Intention is one of the keys to successful Contemporary Seidr work. If you set an intention before you begin and use it as a touchstone throughout you should achieve your goal.

At this point your intention should be simple. Something along the lines of "I'm going to hold on to this state of consciousness for five minutes." Try it. See if you get results.

Set a timer for five minutes. Use your phone or a simple kitchen timer. Now do your thing to get you to that altered state of mind. See if you can hold it for five minutes. It's hard at first. But I never said this was going to be easy! We're looking for progress not perfection. If you can't hold it five minutes, try one. Again, set a timer. You'll get the hang of it soon.

Practice this skill until you're able to hold it for the full five minutes. Straight through. Once you've accomplished that set the timer for ten minutes. Then fifteen. And so on until you're able to stay in this new state of consciousness for 20 to 30 minutes. That's all the time you'll need for a successful Contemporary Seidr session. Anything longer than that just means you haven't set a clear enough intention for a session. More on intention soon!

As you've discovered by now this is a skill that requires practice and patience. I know I needed it when I first started! I had so many false starts for several months that I'm surprised I didn't just give up. Perseverance is a needed skill in this work.

Try to set aside 30 minutes a day to practice these techniques. Try to do it at the same time every day. Right when you wake up or right before you go to bed are perfect. Or when you first get home from work or right after dinner. But experiment with the time of day you do it. Figure out what works best for you and go with it. Everyone's different.

Work on this skill until you're able to hold on for 20 minutes or so. It won't take as long as you may think to achieve this goal. Soon small gains are going to start to grow into big gains. Then you'll be able to move on!

Intention

What is meant by intention? Intention is a stating of your goal for a session of work. It is something that should be simple. Right now, the only intention you should be concerned with is that of holding on to the working trance state of mind. But soon you'll want bigger intentions.

Ultimately your intention will be something like "I'm going to Asgard to speak with Odin." But for now, trust me that your intention should remain small. It's best to build a strong foundation to build upon from the outset. No need to jump ahead. You'll get there!

Intention should always be considered before starting a session. You should have a clear goal in mind. Otherwise you'll just be floundering about the Nine Realms with no purpose. And that's not the point of Contemporary Seidr. Contemporary Seidr should be like surgery. Precise. With a clear intention of the desired outcome.

Intention is the framework upon which you'll build your session. It will serve as a touchstone of sorts. Suppose you're in a trance session humming merrily along and you suddenly realize you've lost your way. Simply restate your intention to yourself and that should get you back on track easily.

Is having an intention just telling myself what I want and then getting it? Isn't this just exercising my imagination then? Nope. You are going to leave yourself open to whatever messages you receive in whatever form during a session. Having an intention isn't about predicting an outcome. It's setting a goal. How that goal is achieved is up to the multiverse.

Goals are important in Contemporary Seidr work. With goals we are able to perform a large variety of tasks. Say you want to perform a healing or visit a departed loved one. Both are worthy goals. And by setting that goal straight away you are more likely to have success at the task at hand.

This aspect of Contemporary Seidr is so important that once you've started practicing it this will become second nature. Just like rhythmic breathing or grounding. Of all the skills you will learn by studying this book, this is one of the most important.

Intention is a focal point in all magical or esoteric work. It is through intention that our will for something is expressed. In the case of Seidr, our will should always be for the best possible outcome of a situation. Say you're journeying to gain wisdom. That wisdom should ultimately be used for the betterment of your clan or yourself. That's a valid intention. Anything dark or potentially dangerous is not in my opinion a worthwhile intention. There's enough bad stuff in our world. Why add to it?

Speaking of bad stuff. Now is as good a time as any to mention protection. You'll be going off to different Realms that sometimes have not nice inhabitants. So, some protection is called for. One of the easiest ways I know to protect yourself is to imagine yourself in a box constructed of window screen material. It will serve to help keep the harmful stuff away but still let the messages get through. Some imagine themselves in coats of armor. But really all I find necessary is along with your intention state that nothing ill will befall you on this journey. I've found for myself that that's enough.

Intention without expectation of the outcome is ultimately what we want. Setting a clear intention without telling the multiverse what the definitive outcome will be; a worthy goal.

Get a map!

In order to travel or journey somewhere new it's always helpful to have a map to get you there. Or a GPS. But even a GPS has to have the information ready to give out. So, before you start journeying let's get a map!

I'm going to ask you now to create a map of the Norse Nine Realms. They are out there just waiting to be discovered by you. Maybe think of yourself as an astronaut charting unseen lands out in space. It's really kinda like that. So, you are now a bold adventurer charting new dimensions. Pretty cool huh?

The Nine Realms in the Norse cosmology are as follows. Midgard is where we live. It is middle earth. It is the home of mundane concerns. Asgard is the home of the Aesir who are the primary gods like Odin and Thor. It is our higher consciousness. For more information about the gods read the "Prose Edda" by Snorri Sturluson. Ljossalfheim is the realm of the light elves. It is the home of intellect. Svartalfheim is the home of the dwarves and home to emotions. Vanaheim is home of the Vanir who are the other clan of gods besides the Aesir. Here we find balance. Muspellheim is the land of fire. It signifies expansive energy. Nifleheim is the world of ice and our contractive energies. Jotunheim is the land of giants or primary elemental forces. Hel is the land of the dead. It houses our subconscious.

Your task is to map these Realms for yourself. You can do some research to get an idea of the maps of others through a quick Google search. But the challenge is to come up with a map of your own.

Get into a working trance using whatever method you have found to be most effective for you. Use the intention of "I am making a map of the Nine Realms." Keep yourself open to whatever information is given to you. Make sure you have your journal handy to draw the map as it comes to you. Do this until you have a complete map of the multiverse.

Don't be surprised if you spontaneously travel to one or more of the Realms by accident. It often happens while doing this exercise. Just don't hang out there. Yet. Make a note in your journal of where it is and move on. Remember your intention is to create a map. Not experience the Realms. That comes soon.

Some people find it easier to create the map in 3D. I had an apprentice who used her son's Tinker Toys for this purpose. Another did it with toothpicks and marshmallows. If it works better for you that way great. Do it that way.

Now you have your map. You have charted where you're going. Time to travel!

First journey

The time has finally come for your first official journey. You know how to get into a working trance. You have your map. You're ready!

To approach this journey, review your map. Get to know where things are in relationship to each other. Get to know the lay of the land. Memorize it as best you can. This first journey will be to Asgard. So, get familiar with that the most.

Asgard is the home of the Aesir. The primary gods. Odin. Thor. Tyr. The big guns. So, we'll want to visit there first. How you experience it will be highly personal. I experience it as a large flat grassy plain with a couple of trees. One of my apprentices experiences it as a Viking Village filled with people. It will really be your experience. Keep yourself open to whatever comes your way.

Ground yourself before this and every journey you take. Focus on the intention "I'd like to visit Asgard." Or something like that. But keep it simple. Now go into your working trance with your intention in mind. This mission should take no more than 15 to 20 minutes. You could even set a timer.

Keeping your intention firmly in mind and your channels as open as they can be and allow yourself to experience whatever happens. It could be something strong and profound. It could be nothing! If you don't have success this first try, simply make another attempt later. There should be no pressure to perform. Pressure brings about bleed-throughs of imagination. And you want an authentic experience.

Remember the images you get may vary. It could be like a 3D movie. It could be colors. It could be sounds. All of these are valid messages. Just allow yourself to experience them.

In this first journey we are not trying to meet any of the entities that dwell there. So, don't expect a chat with Odin your first time out. That will come. The purpose of this first journey is just to get used to how you experience things. That's enough for a good first journey!

Write everything down in your journal. Be as detailed as possible. This will help you build skills for communicating things to others when you do a Contemporary Seidr session for someone else. Remember we are learning all types of new skills. Remain open to it all!

Once the images have stopped coming or your timer goes off it's time to get out of trance. Focus yourself on your ordinary consciousness. The room you're in. The light source. The noises that you hear more distinctly now. Slowly reacclimatize to the world around you. Getting out of trance should be as gradual a process as going into one. But as you have kept your consciousness involved on some level to the mundane it will not be as shocking as just simply snapping out of trance.

Congratulations! You have completed your first journey. Hopefully it was fun! Hopefully you took all kinds of notes on your experience. Hopefully it wasn't too difficult. Ready for more?

More journeying

Hopefully by now you've had a successful journey to Asgard. That leaves eight more Realms to visit! So that's what you'll do next.

Prepare by looking at your map. Pick a Realm to go to. Do your grounding and protection work. Get into a working trance using whatever method you prefer. Set your intention. Say it's Vanaheim you intend to visit. Set your intention of something along the lines of "I will visit Vanaheim".

Something to think about when setting intention. Keep them positive and proactive. Try not to use words like "wish". Use the word "will". That way you will be sending out into the multiverse the notion that is will be done. A small thing but keeping things as direct and positive can really make a big difference in your success.

While traveling to these Realms there are some things to consider. The purpose of this set of exercises is not to chat with any of the entities that live there. That will come. If you're approached by someone don't be rude. But interactions with entities is not the goal. Interact with the environment.

Try to capture as many details about the Realm as you can. What is the landscape like? How about temperature? Can you hear any sounds? Is it sunny or overcast? Every detail you collect is important. Again, we're building the skill of being able to recount to others what you've experienced in as detailed a manner as possible.

Come out of trance gently. Write everything you've experienced in your journal. And do this for each of the remaining Realms. Not terribly difficult is it?

This process should take over a week to accomplish. You only want to do one session a day. Otherwise you run the risk of becoming "trance drunk". It is possible to become addicted to experiencing the other Realms of reality over ordinary consciousness. This could lead to a psychotic break. Not something to mess with. And don't try to string visiting more than one Realm in a session. You'll burn out. Try to keep in mind that this is not a game. This is serious stuff not to be taken on as a lark. A little caution goes a long way. And that's for the good.

Remember if at first you don't succeed… Try as many attempts as it takes to visit each Realm. There's no need to rush. You'd rather have quality sessions than not. So, if it takes you a couple of tries to achieve a goal so what? Who's watching?

This series of exercises should really get your trance skills into order. After visiting the Nine Realms you will have an idea of what works best for you and what doesn't. Just take your time and make sure your outcomes are fitting your desires. Simple. But complicated…

Time to chat

By now you have visited all Nine Realms and have a pretty good idea of what to expect in each one. If you have any doubts about the validity of your discoveries always double check with the lore. It's a great way to let yourself be at ease and confident that what you're experiencing is true. Can't hurt!

Now it's time to go back and have a few chats with folks. Take a journey to each Realm with the intention of "I will talk to Odin in Asgard" for example. Remember to keep your intention clean and simple. Also don't forget to make it a verification of the intent.

What do you wish to gain? Any wisdom they have to impart to you. Wisdom and knowing are all hallmarks of the entities to be found in the Nine Realms. Time to pick some brains.

Each entity you approach will have a different style of speaking. Some will be direct. Some will be flowery. Some will speak in riddles. Just as in ordinary consciousness not everyone speaks the same way. So, it is in the world of trance. Always keep yourself as open as possible to receive the wisdom shared. And don't get mad if it's not what you wanted to hear. Sometimes wisdom in the form of truth may hurt.

Before you make these journeys, you may want to do some reading of the lore to prepare yourself. For example, if Frigga appears to you as a man you're probably not speaking to Frigga! A simple reading of the ways others have experienced these entities before will again help you understand what is a valid experience.

Your results may vary from other's experience. Drastically. But by now you should have something of an internal truth detector to help you know what's true for you.

UPG or unverified personal gnosis is territory of all of our work. While we can certainly do some research on what we've seen and heard nothing beats that gut feeling you get when something is true. But be warned if you think you're in Muspellheim and it's covered over with ice you're probably in Niflheim. Just huge discrepancies such as that should be a warning for you. If you experience something totally beyond the realm of traditional knowledge and your gut says that it's true take a day or so and go back and revisit the entity in question in another session. If you get the same results, it means it's true. For you. What is true for others may vary widely. And that's great! It's part of what makes this work interesting.

By the time you've completed this exercise you should have a truly solid trance life going on. If not or you're still feeling a bit shaky go back to the basics and try again. The only one you have to report to is yourself.

The next two chapters will deal with journeying to Niflheim and Hel. Here we go!

Talking to a frost giant

We're going to talk about your journey to Niflheim to chat with an entity there. Approach this journey with a sense of purpose and also a sense of fun. Journeying should never be a chore. It should always be a joy.

Do all your preparations for trance. Light candles and incense if you do so. Get in your comfy seat. Pull out your drum if you use one. Get out your map. Set your intention of something like "I am traveling to Niflheim to talk with someone for wisdom." Of course, as always do your grounding and protecting. And off we go!

This journey to seek wisdom in Niflheim is all about mist. The mentions found in the lore state that this is a land of mist. And ice. It is one of the first realms created. Ginnungagap got the two elements of ice and fire together to create the multiverse. Muspellheim being fire. So, the creatures you'll encounter there are very ancient indeed. And with age comes wisdom. So you should get some good stuff here.

Once you've arrived as always in travel get yourself acclimated to the environment. Note the temperature. The landscape. If you see beautiful manicured lawns and it's warm you've arrived someplace other than Niflheim!

Allow yourself to become aware of life forms. Be open to meeting anyone who's there. It will most likely be a frost giant. Don't be scared. If you've done your protection work, you will be fine. If approached by someone who is aggressive, simply state you're here seeking wisdom. Shout it if you have to. In all my journeys and I've done a few I've never been attacked or injured. Don't go looking for trouble and you are likely not to find it.

Ask the entity for any wisdom they're willing to share. It may not come to you in words. It may come to you in sounds or feelings. If it is words don't be surprised if they're slow in being uttered. Remember we're dealing with ancient beings. Their sense of time is very different from ours. Always be respectful and never impatient. You're on their turf. Keep that in mind.

Never fear that you're invading someone else's Realm. For the purposes we're going there for it's not really an intrusion. Or gods forbid an invasion. Go in with that attitude and you're bound to have trouble. Humble and respectful are the best states of mind to be in when journeying. Get cocky and you're in for a bad time.

After they've told you their wisdom be sure to thank them and make your return to ordinary consciousness. This is the time to write it all down in your journal. And congrats! You've just had a successful journey to seek wisdom. Take a moment to reflect on your feelings about this. I would hope you would have a sense of excitement. And be proud of yourself. This is some major work you're doing. Let that all sink in. And continue to enjoy the feelings of satisfaction that come from a job well done.

Go to Hel!

It's time to travel to Hel. Not hell. Hel. The Norse Realm for rest. This Realm has nothing in common with the Christian version. So, there's nothing to fear.

I experience Hel as a kind of desert. Dry and hot. But not open flames or anything. A place of quiet and rest. But hot. That's how it appears to me. You may have a totally different take on it. As ever remain open.

You begin this journey as you do all journeys. By doing what you need to do to get yourself into a working trance. Breathe. Drum. Chant. Sway. Whatever you have discovered works for you.

Set your intention as something like "I'm going to travel to Hel." Again, keep it simple and straightforward. Then you're on your way!

One thing to keep in mind on a trip to Hel is that you're going to want to bring meat with you to offer Garm. He's the nasty guard dog of Hel. He may be nice to Hella but you're going to want to offer him a distraction. Meat does nicely in my dealings with him.

Once there call out for Hella the goddess of the Underworld. She responds rather quickly for me when I go. See how she appears to you. For me it's the traditional view of half beautiful woman half decaying corpse. Allow yourself a moment to grow accustomed to her. She does take some getting used to.

Here's where this journey differs a bit from the others you've taken. As opposed to asking Hella for wisdom you're going to ask her to speak with one of your ancestors. They will offer you the wisdom this time. Don't be specific about which ancestor to talk with this first time out. Remain open to whichever ancestor wishes to speak with you. You'd be surprised how many of them will have something to offer you. But make sure you state to Hella you wish to speak to one ancestor. No need to cause a stampede!

Tell whatever ancestor appears that you have come seeking wisdom. Allow them a chance to answer you fully. They may be quite long winded. Or they may offer you only one word. Take what they offer and thank them. Then return as always to ordinary consciousness. Write it all down in your journal. And that's it!

This is a journey you will want to take frequently. There are a lot of ancestors with a lot of knowledge to share. I use this as one of my go to Contemporary Seidr sessions for this very reason. It never fails that someone has something good to tell me.

It's because of this work that Contemporary Seidr workers should build a strong relationship with Hella. It may take some time. I worked diligently for six months to build my relationship with her. But it was time well spent to be sure.

At this point you should be traveling the Nine Realms with greater ease. You should have a solid working trance down pat. It's now that the real fun begins...

Contemporary Seidr and Runes

Contemporary Seidr and the Runes are the two main arms of the Esoteric Norse pagan body. Each relies on different aspects of brain work to succeed in my experience. Contemporary Seidr and the Runes work from different sides of the brain. Contemporary Seidr relies on the intuitive or right side of the brain. The Runes are part of the analytical or left side of the brain. But what happens when they are combined? Can they actually work together to create positive useful experiences? Let's take a look.

One of the easiest ways to combine these two disciplines is to use one to clarify or underscore the other. This works wonders in helping to get a new perspective on a Contemporary Seidr session or Rune reading. Have a confusing Contemporary Seidr session? Get some additional insight with a Rune reading. Rune reading got you flummoxed? Why not turn to Contemporary Seidr for a second opinion?

The easiest way to get a fix on a troublesome Rune reading is to go into a working trance. Concentrate on the Runes in the reading and as your intuitive side will be open you will receive information you might not have gotten in ordinary consciousness. It certainly works for me.

And if a Contemporary Seidr session has got you confused use the Runes for additional insight into the meaning. By using the more logical side of your brain things can easily be made concrete that seemed too Esoteric or vague. This also works well for me.

These two disciplines work so well this way simply because they act from different sides of our brains. Together they combine in simple but powerful ways to work a double whammy on any Esoteric problem.

Another way to use them together is to "ride the energy" of the Runes into a Seidr state. Each separate Rune has an energy attached to it. Unique to themselves. I experience these energies almost as a frequency like a radio signal. I tap into the vibrations and "tune" them like a radio. Then I can "ride" the frequency all the way into a trance state.

Particularly good for this technique are the Runes ehwaz, eiwaz and raidho. Ehwaz for the horse riding aspect. Eiwaz for the yew tree Yggdrasil that we travel up and down for journeying. And raidho for the cart or journey meanings. These Runes stand out as tools to facilitate journey.

Some people experience these different frequencies as colors. These folks experience the frequency of the individual Runes in visual form. They are then able to concentrate on a particular Rune color and get into trance in part that way. Contemporary Seidr skills are broad in their ability to be applied.

Another way to use these two branches of the same tree together is to go into a working trance to do all of your rune readings. I do this all the time. The results may startle you. In a working trance your intuitive right brain side is wide open and receptive. It may allow you access to meanings and patterns that you otherwise might not have seen. I know I have had some eye-opening realizations using this method. It should work for you as well.

These are just a few of the ways Contemporary Seidr and Runes can be used in tandem. Remember to always remain open to innovation. This work is all about new explorations. Let your imagination soar! Imagination is not a dirty word in this work. It is a tool needed to get us over a few bumps and allow us to take action when called for. Keep that in mind as you move forward. And for the gods' sake keep moving forward whatever the price!

Contemporary Seidr and the gods

One thing my experiences in this path has taught me is that it's a lot easier to do this work if you do it with the gods beside you. Including the gods into your Contemporary Seidr work brings new life into the proceedings. In my experience you can see more and travel deeper with the assistance of the gods.

Which gods? For me there is a grouping of three deities that I work closely with during my Contemporary Seidr sessions.

First is Freyja. Freyja is by most accounts in the lore the go to goddess of this work. I certainly have found that to be the case. In my workings with Freyja I call upon her with chant while drumming. Soon enough she normally appears. And if she intends to help me with journeying, she brings her boar. As she rides up and makes herself known to me, I get the tingling sensation that something is about to happen. This generally takes the form of a sensation in my head. It feels like a cold wind is blowing. After she arrives, if I am to travel, she gets off her boar and invites me to ride. Then I simply ride the boar to whatever realm I'm to travel to. The ride is normally very quick to happen. That's what happens with me and Freyja. Try contacting her and see if she'll have you ride her boar.

Then there's Odin. He comes next for me. After all Freyja taught him the secrets of Seidr in exchange for knowledge of the Runes. This of course is documented in the lore. The work of Freyja and Odin in the two main branches of heathen Esoterica is the stuff of pure great myth. Two powerhouses exchanging information on magical workings. So, Odin is a major deity in regard to Seidr. I call upon him specifically for journeys to Asgard. It is there that some of the best work to be done is done. But Odin helps steer doings in all the Nine Realms as well as Freyja does. Between the two of them there's pretty much nothing that can't be done.

Lastly is Hella. She is a necessity for working with the ancestors. She holds the key to communication with departed family. By working with her the storehouse of ancestral wisdom is unlocked. And that's big stuff indeed! Working with her was detailed in the chapter on going to Hel. Reread it if you need tips on getting somewhere with Hella.

Working with these three deities will help bring your Contemporary Seidr work to new depth and clarity. Let them serve as your guides to this uncharted territory of the Nine Realms. You could do far worse.

Contemporary Seidr and ritual

Contemporary Seidr and ritual work wonderfully together. Contemporary Seidr can bring new depth to a simple ritual activity. It definitely gives your ritual a focal point and meaning to keep your ritual activity from becoming boring or commonplace. I highly recommend that you try incorporating Contemporary Seidr into your rituals.

How does this work? It's not really difficult once you have the skill set down to enter into trance. Try something along this line and see what results you have.

Start by picking an intention for the ritual and the trance session. Remember to keep it simple. Let's say you're doing a ritual to honor your ancestors.

Dig out your drum if you use one. Start drumming. Call upon the ancestors to be with you. Try for obscure family that you really didn't have much or any contact with during their lifetime. Dig through old family photos for Great Aunt Betsy and see if you can connect with her. Keep her name and if you have one her image solidly in your mind while you drum. Chant her name. Call upon her. Let yourself become immersed in the thought of her.

When you feel her presence strongly go into your trance session. Sway. Drum. Sing. Do whatever you've discovered is the best way for you to get there.

Once you've achieved a trance state look around you. Are the surroundings familiar? A family home where she may have lived? A blank atmosphere with nothing really distinguishing it? Get to know the scenery. Smell the smells. Feel the temperature. Touch things if you'd like. Anything that can assist you in grounding yourself in this place.

Turn to Great Aunt Betsy. Ask her what she would have you know. Don't be surprised by the answers. Sometimes ancestors have some pretty shocking things to say! Allow the time to ask follow up questions if needed. Don't rush things. You bothered to call upon her so let yourself fully experience her wisdom.

Once you have gotten all you think you're going to get from her thank her for her words of wisdom. Switch your thought to exiting the trance. Drum or sing or sway yourself gently back into ordinary consciousness.

Now complete your ritual. Make a toast to Great Aunt Betsy. Make an offering to her. Say aloud your thanks for this opportunity. And you're done!

This is just one example of how to use Contemporary Seidr in ritual. There are many many more. The only limit is the limit of your abilities to imagine. So have some deeper more meaningful ritual work using Contemporary Seidr. You won't ever go back to a humdrum ritual once you have.

Woman's work?

There's a mindset among some folk that Contemporary Seidr is woman's work. I don't agree. Not just because I'm a man who does this work. But because I believe we have evolved past such polarizing attitudes.

It's true that in the lore the most famous Seidr worker was female. The "Saga of Erik the Red" tells the story of a woman who performs a high seat Seidr session with a chorus of females to assist her. But I speak of Contemporary Seidr. This type of work is used and done successfully by members of both sexes. It draws no distinction between the two. My own personal experience with apprentices has shown that men have an interest and talent for this work. So, I say rubbish to those who make distinctions based on gender.

I truly believe this work is to be done by anyone regardless of their gender identity. Today we have a society that includes individuals who identify with a whole range of gender titles. Terms that were never heard of some years back are now commonplace. Cisgender. Gender fluid. These folks who identify on this larger broader spectrum are all part of Contemporary Seidr.

There's a history of gender ambivalence in those who do this kind of work. Take the berdache of Native Americans. They were men who dressed in woman's attire and performed all manner of sacred work. Including journeying. In the Norse tradition men who did this kind of work were considered "ergi". They were the medicine men of their culture. They definitely did trance work.

Today and throughout history men were seers and Seidr workers along the women. Still having trouble accepting this as fact? Here's an exercise to try.

Go into your working trance. Once there call upon a god and goddess to work with. It could be Odin and Freyja. They are the two most closely related to this work. So, they would make great contacts for this purpose. Focus on the energies of the god and goddess you've chosen. It's essential that you keep both deities in mind simultaneously. Then sit back and see how they interact. Do they dance together in front of a bonfire? Do they both drum and chant? Do they work together harmoniously? Now listen for their message to you regarding this issue. Their message may come in the form of words spoken directly to you. Or it may come in the form of their dance. Or perhaps they'll just send you feelings or emotions. Whatever form it takes jot it down in your journal. This is an instance of direct communication from beyond. Then come out of your trance as usual. After thanking the deities of course!

How do you feel about men doing this kind of work now? Has your mind been changed? Have you received further insight on this matter? Do you feel you now can accomplish this work with a more open mind? If so great! If you still have the feeling that men shouldn't be doing Seidr repeat the exercise. Soon enough you'll be transformed.

There is no reason in this day and age why there should be any doubt about men doing trance work. It's an outdated thought pattern. Men and women can equally do this work successfully. That's my take on it. As a Vitki and a Norse Shaman.

Contemporary Seidr as a gateway

Contemporary Seidr should in my opinion never be viewed as a destination. For me it is always a section of my path to further spiritual growth. A valuable part of the journey but by no means a stopping place. Contemporary Seidr serves as a gateway to greater bigger things.

One of the main purposes for practicing Contemporary Seidr is the expansion of your mind and point of view. If you're performing it regularly and with dedication it serves as a window to whole new realms of existence. Not something that is finite but infinite. Door opening to new door. Always a chance to move forward on your spiritual quest. It's one of the main reasons I practice this work. It opens up the multiverse to me in ways I could never have imagined.

One way that Contemporary Seidr has served as a gateway in my practice is the ability to communicate with those who have left this realm for someplace else. Contemporary Seidr allows me a chance to have conversations with my departed parents that I would never have had with them while they were tied to this realm. My father and I had a difficult relationship when he was alive. But in death he's become much more accessible and open to me. He's definitely the same old dad he was before but now his thoughts and responses are more universal and global. He got really smart once he'd died! This is a transformation that I never imaged would be possible. But now my conversations with him while I'm in trace are filled with good advice and a sense of keeping me on my path.

Another thing that Contemporary Seidr has served as a gateway for me in is an understanding of the feminine spiritual side of life. As a man the energy of the feminine had always eluded me. I was great at lists and labels. Not so good at intuition or feelings. But through Contemporary Seidr I have gotten into contact with the feminine side of myself. Opening up to the multiverse regularly and frequently I have learned the skill of trusting my hunches and random thoughts as messages from my divine feminine. This has created a new sense of balance in my life. It has taught me the wisdom and value of the unseen. And it has definitely opened my mind to a whole different kind of reality.

Here is an exercise to try. Go into a working trance with the intention that you will receive wisdom on an area of growth for your personal life. Find out that area and shift your intention to discovering more about this aspect of Self. Look at this aspect while in trance from as many sides and angles that you can. Make notes in your journal of your discoveries. Use those notes for future Seidr sessions on this topic. Soon you'll be opening a whole new realm of your life!

So, in my experience Contemporary Seidr serves as a gateway to even more amazing and wonderful things. I cannot stress how important this is for me in my current daily life. I think with some practice and some time you will find the same is true for you!

Hyde and go fetch

Now is the time we get into the soul work part of Contemporary Seidr. Stay with me folks! Things might get a bit crazy!

In the Norse tradition the soul has nine different aspects or sections. In this exercise and chapter, we will deal with two of them. The hyde and the fetch.

The hyde or hamr is the aspect of the soul that most closely resembles the aura that many people are familiar with. This aspect is almost a second skin for the physical body. In my experience it hovers about an inch above the physical self. It is colored energy. Mine is a purple pink. It is your job to get to know yours and the colors and structure it has. The easiest way to get in touch with your hyde is to lay down and relax. Get yourself into a working trance. Once you've achieved that the work can begin. See with your mind's eye the shape and color of your hyde. Keep yourself open to whatever impressions you may receive. Most people experience their hyde as I've said as a near second skin that hugs their body. It will have a glimmering effect to it as energy comes in and goes out. This is natural. The hyde is a living thing. So, it will not remain set in stone or stagnate. Let yourself send your consciousness into your hyde. Are there any discolored sections or imperfections in the body you're seeing? If so, make note of this. Project as much of yourself as you're able into this energy form. Experience life through your hyde. What impressions do you get? How does it feel to your physical body? What sensations do you receive? These are all things you're going to want to jot down in your journal for later reference. Once you have spent some time with your hyde, it's time to get out of your trance. Do this by taking your consciousness back into your physical form. After coming out of trance, do a grounding session again. You want to make sure you're fully back in the ordinary consciousness.

Once you've become adept at experiencing your own hyde it's time to get to know others on this level. Go into your working trance while you're with another person. See if you can get in touch with their hyde. Again, be on the lookout for discoloration or other seeming imperfections. These will be important when we move along. Remember to always get the permission of the person who's hyde you wish to view. This is a very private aspect of Self to be in contact with. You want to have full disclosure of your intents and methods of achieving them.

The second aspect of the Self we'll deal with now is the fetch or fylgja. This is the aspect on the astral level that is sent forth to do work you cannot do. The fetch is generally in the shape of a person of the opposite gender from you. Sometimes they appear in the shape of an animal. You can have more than one fetch at any given time. The point of the fetch is that you are going to be sending them forth into the multiverse to do work.

The best way I have found to discover your fetch is to go into a working trance with the intention of meeting your fetch. Allow yourself to remain open to any insights you may gain. See if your fetch takes the form of a person or animal. Either way they are the aspect of yourself that you are going to send out. Once you've made contact with your fetch try putting as much of your consciousness into it as you can. The ability to see, smell, taste and feel are all important attributes to have in your fetch. Once you're satisfied that as much of your consciousness as you're able is in your fetch try sending it out. See if it will travel throughout the multiverse through your fetch. See if you can maintain all of your senses in the fetch as it travels. Note as you travel any impressions you may get. Is the temperature different than where your physical body is? Are there colors or smells that you come in contact with? Remember to write all of this in your journal. Once you've traveled via your fetch bring your awareness back into your body. Ground yourself after. There. You've just sent part of your consciousness out into the world to experience things you can't in ordinary consciousness. You should feel pretty good about that!

So that is your fetch and your hyde. Hone these skills in contacting and using them. You will be using these skills later.

Contemporary Seidr and the lyke

On to another one of the nine aspects of the Norse soul. The lyke. The lyke is your physical body. That which can be seen and manipulated in ordinary consciousness. It is the vehicle we use to do all our work. And as such we need to keep it humming at its optimal best.

The first thing to consider in regard to your lyke and this work is grounding. This is a vital part of the practice of any Contemporary Seidr worker. Being properly grounded can mean the difference between a successful Contemporary Seidr session and a fiasco. By rooting yourself firmly in the earth you are able to draw upon great reserves of energy. That way you won't be exhausting yourself needlessly. The energy of the earth in itself is a grounding device. It is strong. Solid. It offers you all you need in the way of energy for a bang-up session. Use it to avoid feeling totally drained after you do your work.

Eat something after. I keep candy bars on hand for this. And okay I just like candy bars! But this small amount of food after a session will also help to keep you grounded in ordinary consciousness after a big journey. Protein also works very well for this. Even a couple of slices of cheese can make a world of difference.

Do some light exercise. This will also help ground you. It also serves as a way to get the blood flowing before a session. This will also help with your endurance. There are some sessions that take a long time! You'll want to be certain your vehicle doesn't give out before you're done!

This next paragraph is totally my own opinion formed after years of experience. Take it with a grain of salt. Another thing to consider when talking about the lyke is keeping your channels clear. For me this means no mind-altering substances. At least not the day you journey. Pot and alcohol are fine but in regard to our work they tend to muddy up the channels used for success. Why?

Because these substances alter your mind's ability to work at peak condition. I know there are those who use mushrooms and the like to journey. To me that seems like cheating. I don't like to have any crutches in my Seidr practice. I get fine results without the chemical assistance. So before turning to a mind-altering chemical do yourself a favor and really try to do trance without it. In a worst-case scenario try them if you feel you have used up every other method.

These are some quick examples of working with your lyke in regard to Contemporary Seidr. Take these little tips and see where they lead you!

Contemporary Seidr and odr

Odr is another of the nine aspects of the Norse soul. It translates loosely into the inspiration of your being. It is not always just a flash of inspiration that hits you suddenly. It can be a source of power that you can access at any time you find you need it. Here's an exercise to help you get better in touch with this aspect of your soul.

Do your working trance process. Light incense. Drum. Sway. Whatever it takes till you feel that shift in your consciousness. Once there get in touch with your hyde or hamr. Feel it. And then become aware of a glowing white ball of light at the center of your forehead. Feel your way into this ball of energy. Allow yourself to be a part of this energy. This is your odr.

Once you are familiar with the energy situated at the center of your forehead make the ball grow larger. You can do this by filling it more and more with energy from the earth. If you're properly grounded this should be an easy task. Make the ball so full of energy and large enough that it covers your entire body. Allow some time in this state. Remain open to whatever messages you may receive from the multiverse. Write down in your journal any ideas or images that may come to you. Hopefully the thoughts will be flying and you may have difficulty keeping up. That's fine. That's odr at work. Just jot down what you can. Remember you can repeat this exercise as often as you wish for another infusion of inspiration. Once you feel you've had enough shrink the white ball back to its place at the center of your forehead. Slowly regain a sense of ordinary consciousness. And it's as easy as that!

As I said this exercise can be done as often as needed. I always do this before I write. You could do it before a big meeting at work to come up with some terrific ideas to present. Wow the boss with your odr! There really is no limit to how this energy can be used. Tapping into the thread of the multiverse that serves to inspire you can only have beneficial results.

That's a way to explore the odr. Keep this tool in your toolbox for those times when you need an added umph of inspiration. It's never failed me yet! May it serve you as well.

Contemporary Seidr and the hamingja

The hamingja is one of the Norse nine aspects of Self. Simply put the hamingja is ancestral luck. How often have you heard "That family is cursed!" or "Everyone in that family does so well!"? This is the hamingja at work. There is a clear connection between you and your ancestors regarding the amount and kind of "luck" you have. The question you need to ask yourself is whether or not you'd like to strengthen those bonds or cut yourself off from them.

We all have family traits that seem to be prevalent in our own kin. Whether it be a green thumb or the specter of alcoholism there are definitely aspects of our lives that seem to be handed down. The hamingja rules this type of luck. Here's how you can boost it or remove its influences.

First you need to find out how you experience your own personal hamingja. Go into a working trance with the intention of finding your hamingja. Become aware of your hyde or hamr. Explore this for your hamingja. I experience mine as almost a collar of energy around my neck. Mine is green in color. You may discover yours in a different place and different color. Remain open to any information you may receive. Once you have discovered your hamingja it's time to do some further exploration.

While still in your working trance think of your father of your mother. If they have passed over send explorative threads of energy from your hamingja to reach theirs in the other Realms. If they are still alive, you will do the same, but it should be simpler to accomplish as you know where geographically they are. If you are adopted it's a greater challenge. Just keep your intention on finding your parent's hamingja. It's up to you to do the exploration necessary to make this working successful.

Once you have sent tendrils from your hamingja to those of your parent's, what you do next will depend on whether you wish to make the connections stronger or cut back on them. You should be able to see tendrils from your parent's hamingja to your hamingja. These will either be bright in color or dark. The bright are naturally the positive aspects and the dark are the negative. What you can do now is send a hook of energy into the bright connections to boost your luck and sever the dark connections to end a negative influence. And that should do it!

You can go back even further to grandparents and great grandparents. In blended families it is important that you stick with your bloodline. However, if you're in a blended family or adopted you can do this work with anyone who was an important influence on your life. Do some Esoteric research in the other Realms to figure out your parentage if you haven't got a clue.

All of this takes some practice. I recommend trying out each step of the sequence separately before you string it all together in one long session.

This technique has worked for me and several of my apprentices. The trick is to work your way up to one big session after doing each of the steps building onto each other. And don't expect a result if you only do it once. Work this big requires some repetition. I recommend doing the full exercise nine times for the best effect. Does it matter whether you focus on your mother's or father's side? Not really. All that matters is that you remain focused on the working while you do it. Use this technique to create some true change in your life!

Contemporary Seidr and healing

Now that you've gotten in touch with your hyde and fetch it's time to put that knowledge to work. One of the most profound ways you can do this is in healing work. Healing work allows you the opportunity to be of service to your clan and tribe in a big way. No small potatoes this skill...

First, we'll talk about how to heal yourself. The best way I have found to do this is to go into a working trance. Once there get in touch with your hyde. Really remain open to this. Take a look around. Look for any discoloring or gaps in your hyde. These are the areas you'll need to address. Now focus on a problem area. Send energy from the earth (you remembered to ground yourself before you started right?) into the troubled area. Keep sending energy from the earth into this area until its color is the same as the rest of your hyde. Or until the gap is filled. Once you're happy with that fill your entire hyde with energy until it is glowing and filled with a sense of light. Do this ritual frequently as we all tend to backslide in this regard. Once you've healed yourself in this manner you can begin the work of healing others.

Now it's time to work with someone else. This is what you can do if the person you're healing is able to physically be in the same space as you. Have the person get into a comfortable position. I find it easiest to work on others if they're laying down. But sitting in a comfortable chair can work just as well. Have the person focus on their breathing. Have them do the four in four hold four out method to get their breathing into a rhythm. This is to relax them and help open them up to the work you're about to do. Once they're relaxed go into your working trance. Once you're there begin by sending your consciousness out toward the other person. Get in touch with their hyde. Again, get to know it. Look for blemishes or gaps. As above fill the areas with energy you draw up from the earth. Allow ample time to achieve this goal. Once you have done this work and their hyde is complete again you should draw your consciousness back into yourself. Allow the other person some time to get themselves back to a sense of breathing naturally. This work is now done. Congrats! You've just helped another person to live a better life!

Now it's time to tackle the challenge of healing someone over a distance. This is where your fetch comes into play. I find that in my practice most of my healing work falls into this category. It's really no different from doing this work with someone who is physically in the same space as you. Only now you're going to send your fetch out to do the work. Before beginning, you'll need to gather some information from the person you'll be doing the healing for. Where do they live? What do they look like? When is the best time to do the healing when they'll be able to achieve a relaxed state for healing to occur? Once you've settled all that begin your work at the agreed upon time. Here's where the fun comes in. Get yourself into a working trance and connect with your fetch. Send your consciousness into the fetch. Once you've done that send your fetch off to find the person you're healing. This can take some time. Using the information given to you by the other person look for them in the astral plane. If you can ask the person to send a beacon of energy out at the appointed time. Once your fetch has found the other person it's the same drill as healing someone who's physically with you. Look for imperfections in their hyde. Fill with energy taken from the earth. I admit it's challenging to get all these balls into the air at once. It is a bit of a juggling act. But you can do this! Always follow up a distance healing session with a phone call getting the other person's impressions of how it all went on their end. Sometimes they'll actually be able to report seeing or sensing your fetch being with them. Other times it may be a sense of heat or tingling. But hopefully they've felt something. Now you've done distance healing!

I've provided you with the skeleton of how to do this work. Now it's time for you to give it flesh and blood. For example, how exactly do I get my consciousness into my fetch to send it forth? I could tell you but that would rob you the chance to discover it on your own. This needs to be a personal practice. Only trial and error will give you those answers. So practice! Remember much of this work is experimentation. Try methods out to see what works best for you. This is your practice. Don't let me or anyone else tell you there's only one way to do it. This whole book is written in that spirit.

These are the three main ways to do healing. As with everything practice makes perfect. So, do as much of this work as you can. And now you're a healer. Feels good huh? Now you can be of service. There is no higher calling for a Contemporary Seidr worker.

Down time

You've been at this for awhile. Everything has been moving along swimmingly. But suddenly it doesn't work. So, you try again. Still nothing. You start getting concerned. What's going on? Nothing. Literally. You're just experiencing some down time.

Down time is not a bad thing. It gives you a chance to recharge your batteries. It gives you a chance to reflect on your progress to date. It allows you some freedom too. You now have a chance to explore.

Try different ways to get into your working trance. If you haven't used them try drumming. Try scent. Try swaying. All those different ways to journey are available to you. Use them.

The thing about coming up with different ways to travel is that it makes you a stronger Contemporary Seidr worker. These different paths are all tools for your toolbox. If one doesn't work, try another. You'll open yourself up to an array of possibilities you may have never imagined. This is the whole point of Contemporary Seidr. Being as open as you can. Only when you're open can the multiverse send stuff your way. And that's one of the keys to Contemporary Seidr. This is how you experience the marvels of the multiverse. And really isn't that why we do this work in the first place?

I have these spells often. When they first popped up, I tried to force my way through them. I doubled down my efforts to trance. I tried doing it a couple of times a day. I figured I could force a solution. This of course is the exact opposite of what I should have done. Dry patches don't require more effort. They need more relaxation. I know that now. And now so do you!

I knew a Volva who said that during these spells she just grabs a beer and lets it roll. Exactly the correct approach! So, when you have these things happen to you don't worry about it. Relax. Try new ways to approach the work. And most importantly don't give up! Let it ride!

Contemporary Seidr and emotion

All Esoteric work is or can be fueled by emotion. Emotion is a powerful tool to keep in your toolbox. An emotion like love can be the added umph to take a session to a whole new level. Same with an emotion like hate.

Love and Contemporary Seidr work well together. Say you're doing a session to travel to Hel to meet with an ancestor. You can approach this task from a totally neutral place emotionally and get some results. Or you could approach it with a sense of love and get even better results.

Go about it this way. Fill your consciousness with feelings of love. Think of all the good memories you may have of that ancestor. Or if you didn't know them personally fill your mind with feelings of love and gratitude for all that the ancestor went through in their life. With a little practice it shouldn't be difficult for you to come up with ways to drum up a little love. Or a lot.

Once you're feeling the love go into your working trance. Keep the emotion at the back of your mind while you do this. The emotion you're feeling should be easy to send out into the multiverse.

Your good feelings will act as a type of magnet drawing those you wish to interact with to you. This is the added umph I spoke of. Now you've sent out a positive beacon for those ancestors you wish to meet. They will be drawn to the emotion and want to talk to you. And voila! Mission accomplished.

Hate can be used as well. Although it's trickier. Hate can act as a repellent thwarting your intention of the session. But it's worked for me. Sometimes. So, give it a try.

Again, fill yourself with emotion. This time it's negative thoughts you want to fill yourself with. Really work yourself up into a lather. Then go into your working trance. Hopefully you'll find that sending out a strong emotion will again act as a magnet. There are those that are drawn by the dark. But don't be surprised if you're attempt is not as successful. Those who in life were drawn to the darker side of things will often take the bait. As always experiment with this. See what kind, if any, results you get. Those who in life were covered in darkness often find this strong emotion irresistible.

There are mentions in the lore where hate is used by a Seidr worker to bring about change. One of the most known is the infamous nidstang pole of the Egil Saga. As I tend to view myself personally as a positive Vitki and keep my work as positive as possible I don't tend to go the curse route. But it's there and can be used. A little research into the lore will make that application apparent.

Another emotion to work with is joy. As above, fill yourself with joyous thoughts. Send that out into the multiverse as you go into your working trance. This method is especially good if you don't have a specific goal in mind and just want to journey for the Hel of it. Keeping yourself joyful again will act as a magnet. See who responds!

Hopefully this has shown you the power of emotion in Contemporary Seidr. Experiment. Always stay open. And of course, always keep trying!

Contemporary Seidr and time travel

We've already proven you can do travel among spaces through your fetch. So now the question is can you actually travel through time with Contemporary Seidr? I tell you that indeed you can. Here's how.

Choose an event from your life that still brings up strong negative feelings for you. Remember as much of the event as you can in your ordinary consciousness.

Then do your working trance stuff. The intention that you will use as a focus is that you're going to travel to talk with Freyja. Once in your trance look for and send out the intention that you'd like to speak with Freyja. She will probably be found in Asgard. Once you've established a connection with her the work can begin.

Tell her about your memory. Ask her if she will assist you in rewriting the memory so that it no longer brings you pain. Why Freyja? She is the goddess of Seidr. Who better to help you?

Mentally bring Freyja back to the memory. Allow it to play out as you recall it having occurred. At this point ask Freyja to change the memory so it is no longer painful. She could do a few things. She could show you the memory through another person's eyes. By doing this the pain may be removed. She may totally rewrite the scene so it has a different ending. Trust that whatever she chooses to do will work.

Once she's done the work at hand thank her and come out of trance. Once back in ordinary consciousness give the memory a test drive. See if the memory still gives you pain. In my experience the memory no longer holds the same power. It's ability to cause pain is removed. That's all there is to it. You have time travelled into the past and affected it in a way that impacts your present.

Freyja may send you to the Norns to do this work. They are also powerful allies in time travel. And they can actually reweave your Wyrd so that the memory no longer exists.

Does this really work? I have used this technique myself. I had a lot of painful memories from my childhood and early adult years. They plagued me. They keep me firmly rooted in the past and unable to move forward with my life in meaningful ways. I used this technique. Sometimes Freyja showed me the memory through another person's eyes. Sometimes she actually rewrote the whole memory so that it was pleasant for me. Either way I found that if that memory would come into my consciousness, it would be in the guise of the new improved version. There was no more pain.

That's how you can time travel using Contemporary Seidr. Perhaps you'll find other ways. Remember to always experiment and keep looking. That's the hallmark of a powerful Contemporary Seidr worker.

Contemporary Seidr and horsing around

Horsing is a technique in which you actually allow a deity to take control of your body and speak through you. You become an instrument for the god to use. Rather like an orchestra instrument is used. It's truly an advanced technique of Contemporary Seidr. But here's how I do it.

Get yourself into a comfortable position. I normally lay down for this work. Do what you've done so far to get yourself into a working trance. This time your intention will be to reach out to the god you'd like to be horsed by. Or if you're feeling very strong just open yourself up to the idea of serving as a horse for whatever deity needs to speak. I generally don't recommend this tactic as you are already giving away so much of your control in this process. I like to have some level of control in my work.

This is kind of work is usually done with witnesses. You want to know what the gods say. Or you could record it if you're flying solo. Either way you'll want a record of the results.

Once in your working trance ask the god you wish to horse for make their presence known. Once you are certain that the deity you desire is with you ask them to horse you. There will be a time of your removing yourself from your body. Send your consciousness out into your hyde or hamr. This is where your consciousness will hang out while the proceeding is happening.

Once you have successfully sent your consciousness into your hyde the god may now enter. For me this always feels like a big bump. Hopefully the transition will be smooth. If not and you feel unsafe or unsure simply end the session; better safe than sorry.

Now the god may speak through you. Try to have a list of questions you'd like answered prepared for this purpose. This will assure that everything you want covered will be. Or else you can just have the general question of what wisdom can the god offer you. This also works well.

Once you've received all the wisdom you can handle it's time to send your consciousness back into your body. Thank the god for allowing you the opportunity to be their instrument. Then send your consciousness back into your lyke. Again, there will probably be a bump as this occurs.

Once back in your body allow yourself to make the trek back to ordinary consciousness. You will most likely be exhausted. And need something to eat. Have something ready so you can just grab it. Allow yourself a moment to really take in what the god has said. Don't be surprised if it's not a clear-cut communication. It may come in the form of riddles. Or it may be in the format of a Q and A session. Be open to whatever ways the deities choose to talk. It may take a while to muddle through. You may have to do a regular Contemporary Seidr session just to get a translation!

As you'll be in a working trance and not totally "under" you maintain a level of control. You can have access to your list of questions and even write down replies. If things get a bit hairy you can simply end the session. These are all ways to maintain control.

I have been doing this process for many years. Only once did I have a situation occur where the god didn't want to leave. If you are in a working trance while you do this and not completely out, you should have no problems. Just remember that you are the one who can send your consciousness out of your hyde and back into your lyke.

That's all there is to horsing for a god. A little intimidating but it can be done. The key is trusting yourself and your skills to actually do it! So, build up your skills and enjoy some horsing around!

Contemporary Seidr and magic

Here's where we'll get into one of my favorite applications of Contemporary Seidr. It's the art of magic. For me much of the value of Contemporary Seidr work lies in its ability to create change in my life. To do that I turn to magic. No not the hocus pocus or Hogwarts type. But rather a full-on way to roll up your sleeves and get things done.

In order to do magic, you first need to figure out what kind of change you'd like to make. This should be a concrete change that you can see the results of in your life.   Something basic. And the more urgent the need for the change the more powerful the magic will be. The sense of urgency will help serve as added energy to the proceedings.

Let's say you'd like to be less fearful in the everyday life. That will be the intention you will send out into the multiverse. It's important that you keep the wording of the sending positive. Positive energy draws more to itself than negative energy does. So keeping the intention positive is important. For this example, you could use "I am less fearful in my life".

Now go into your working trance. Keep your intention in mind as you do this. Be sure to ground yourself well. Once in the trance your magical sending can begin. Travel to Ginnigugnap. The void. It is here in the stillness of nothingness that you can work. Once there pull the energy you have grounded yourself into. See the energy as a form of white light. Draw that light up through your feet, up your legs and up further until it fills your body. Once you feel your body is filled with this energy light focus on the intention of your magical sending.

Once you firmly have the intention in your mind send that intention out through your fingertips into the multiverse. Let the intention ride out in the energy you have filled yourself with. It's kind of like shooting a bow and arrow. It should be that focused and precise. Once you have sent out the intention, send the energy you filled your body with back down your legs and into the earth. The sending is done. Come back into ordinary consciousness.

This same technique can be used with a bind rune. Simply create a bind rune of your desired outcome and send it the same way as above. Then once again come back to ordinary consciousness.

Now you wait. Remember magic doesn't necessarily work instantly. It is not on the same clock we are on. But sooner or later if your sending was successful, you'll feel less fearful. You'll have the courage to do all that you need to do. And it will work on other aspects of your life as well.

I have used this technique myself to great results. I helped myself stay calm in an ongoing personal crisis that I knew wouldn't be resolved immediately. I have used it to get an infusion of cash into my life. All sorts of real-life issues have been addressed through this type of magic. And if it works...

This is a powerful tool for your Seidr worker tool box. Use it well. Practice it. Make positive changes in your life and the sky's the limit!

UPG dude

In case you hadn't noticed by now I'm a UPG dude. Unverified personal gnosis. Having experiences that cannot easily be verified by outside sources. In many ways these experiences make up my practice and teaching in a big way. So what do I do with all of this?

First, I research. Look for matching things in the lore. I'm always amazed that something I've seen or heard in trance can be found in the lore. Or find out if others have had similar experiences. These are both ways to verify what has occurred.

But suppose it's not to be found in the lore no matter how much you scour. Does that make it invalid? I say not. Even if your Seidr buddies have not had similar experiences it could still be true. Remember truth is different for each person. What is true for you may not be true for others.

Which brings us to the question "How do I know it's real?". There are certain ways I know for myself what is real and what is just my imagination. One way I tell is if the experience I had was hyper real or surreal with overly vivid colors. Sounds that are somehow crisper than ordinary consciousness allows. That's how I know it's real. It just feels different from ordinary consciousness. By now you know what I mean. You've been having your own experiences and have a trove of things to compare things to. And through practice and careful journaling you should have an arsenal of material at your disposal. You'll know it's real when it's real.

This very issue is why I don't use mind altering substances to trance. I like to keep my channels clear of obstruction. Even alcohol can block things up. Or make things move too fast. This is definitely a personal choice. But I say why take the chance to mess things up inadvertently?

UPG is a part of the work Contemporary Seidr practitioners do. It won't go away. We just have to learn our own way of handling it.

The best way to get a grip on it is practice. Only through experience will you be able to tell the truth.

Dwarves and Loki

What follows are two techniques to boost the energy available to you for different purposes. They are ways to tap into sources of energy to add momentum to your workings and your physical being.

First up are the dwarves. There are four dwarves stationed one at each point of the cardinal directions. Their names are Nordri (north), Sudri (south), Austri (east), and Vestri (west). It's all there in the Prose Edda of Snorri. These four dwarves are firmly rooted to the ground as they do their work of holding up the multiverse. What better source for long lasting sustained energy than these four?

Go to the center of your private Midgard. Stand there and go into your working trance. Once there hail the four dwarves. Get into contact with each one separately and then try to hold your attention on all four at once. Now become aware of your hyde. Once you've gotten a sense of this glowing energy field send out a tendril of it to one of the dwarves. Dwarves in my experience have hydes like us humans. So, you will be drawing energy directly from the dwarf hyde. Using the tendril from your hyde encircle the dwarf. Connect with its hyde. Feel its strong solid energy. Then draw that energy through the tendril into your hyde. Do this for as long as it feels comfortable. Then take your tendril back into yourself. If needed repeat the above with another of the four dwarves. The key however is to know when you've had enough. This you will learn through practice and trial and error.   Thank the dwarves and come out of trance back into ordinary consciousness

How will you know when you have enough energy? You'll feel a tingling throughout your body. You'll feel wired. Again, the challenge is in knowing when enough is enough. You may get all the energy you need from just one dwarf. It may take all four. Again, trial and error will carry the day.

I have used this technique myself for years. As an MS patient energy levels are a big thing for me. I find that once I've done this exercise, I can face the day more energetically. I also use this exercise to gain energy to use in my magical sendings.

For those who practice chaos magic this next one's for you. Go into your working trance. Travel to Svartalfheim. Find where Loki is bound by the entrails of his offspring on the rock. The energy of Loki is chaotic and dispersed, unlike the strong solid energy of the dwarves. But for some magical sendings this is just the right kind of energy. This energy is great for a working that does not require precision. It's good for sendings that you want dispersed throughout the multiverse. Once you've found Loki you'll probably discover he's writhing to try to free himself. This is the energy you want to tap into. Become aware of your hyde and again send out tendrils to match up with Loki's. Tap into this energy as above and take it into yourself. This energy will feel quite different from the energy of the dwarves. Take in only a little before you draw your hyde back into yourself. Thank Loki for the infusion and come out of trance as always.

Two very different energies for very different purposes. But as ever we want to have as many tools as possible available to us. By now you should have a number of tools ready. But there's never enough!

Contemporary Seidr and ego

Ego is a powerful thing. In the Norse ways it's called Ek. This force can be used for good or bad just like all forces used in Contemporary Seidr.

On the negative side your ego becomes overly inflated. You are doing powerful work indeed when you do Contemporary Seidr work. But we should be mindful that powerful work doesn't turn into a power trip. Just because we are doing big things doesn't make us big. It should make us all the more humble. Seeing firsthand the power and might of the workings of the multiverse seems to remind us that we are indeed small cogs in a huge, wondrous machine. If we are doing our work from a humble place in our minds, we become the oil that keeps the machine running smoothly as well. Work from a place of unmitigated power and you become the gunk in the cogs.

This is the positive side of our work. Using power effectively to make good things happen rather than ill. Staying humble can be a challenge. But it does us no good to walk around telling people you're a powerful Contemporary Seidr worker. Let your deeds speak for you. And may your deeds be all for the betterment of the multiverse.

Doing Contemporary Seidr work for others is a big deal for me. I find great satisfaction using my skills for others. Serving my clan and my tribe helps bring me closer to the gods. And this connection is why I do Contemporary Seidr in the first place. This for me is a humbling event. Being close to the gods I'm reminded of how small I am. A cog in a machine and all.

If you look at it from a different perspective being humble is actually a form of power. In remaining humble you allow yourself to be moved spiritually by all that you experience. And this leads to even greater spiritual strength. Humility is actually a gateway to great power. And I invite you to walk that path.

So be mindful of your Ek. Allow it to remain humble yet powerful. And I know you will have a fuller life as a Seidr worker for the effort.

Contemporary Seidr and song

Song plays a huge part in traditional Seidr. It is the song of the chorus that sends the Volva off into the other Realms. Their songs sing her back into ordinary consciousness. So a big deal. Song can also play a large part in Contemporary Seidr if you so choose. It can be another tool in your Seidr worker toolbox. And the more tools...

One way that song can play an important part in your Contemporary Seidr practice is for you to come up with a song you sing yourself. Make it a simple song that will help send you off to the other Realms. If you drum you can come up with a song with a strong beat that you can strike out on your drum. If you know a traditional language such as German or Icelandic think of writing the song in that language for added authenticity. Really spend some time creating your song. The time you spend on this task can be spent in working trance for greater ease. You can tap into the multiverse that way and if you're really connected the song may practically write itself!

Another approach to song is to chant a song. Again, a drumbeat will greatly assist you in this task. You could try a chant using Runes as in galdr. This will make sure you stay within the Norse template of your practice. I use a simple chant of a series of Runes for this very purpose. I chant the Rune names in the same order every time. This repetition alone can send me off to other Realms. I add some incense and swaying to the proceedings for an extra bump. I stayed away from this particular tool for a long time because I'm not much of a singer! But chanting doesn't require a beautiful voice to be effective. So give this method a try.

Another way to use song in Contemporary Seidr is prerecorded music. There are many available CDs of groups that fit the bill. My first choice in this regard is the band Wardruna. Their music is just the ticket for traveling. I especially like the fact that it's in a language I cannot understand. That way I'm not distracted by listening to lyrics! There are other groups that can serve you just as well in this. Make it a fun adventure to find a group that works for you!

These are some of the ways to use song in Contemporary Seidr. If you find more feel free to let me know. I always love new music!

Contemporary Seidr and the four elements

The four elements that I predominantly work with are earth, air, fire and water. I know there are different opinions on the exact number of the elements and what they are. For my purposes four seems to work best.

The elements are powerful forces to have on your side. They can help you journey as well as they can help in magical work. How do we use the elements in Contemporary Seidr work?

Earth is used as a strong grounding helper. Try going outdoors for your next session. As you begin the process of going into trance and ground yourself, take a minute to really feel the earth beneath you. If you do trance sessions sitting down, feel the earth at the base of your spine. Send your roots down into the ground from that point where your body touches the dirt. This should enable you to ground quite solidly to assist you in your trance work.

Air is relatively simple to access. Get a fan. Electric fans can be used by sitting in front of a running fan and letting yourself focus on the sound and feel of the air rushing by you to carry you into trance. The sound and feel can transport your consciousness rather quickly. Also consider a hand fan like they used before electricity was harnessed. The repetitive motion of using the hand fan along with the feeling of the breeze you're creating can also transport you to an altered state of consciousness.

Fire is up next. Light a candle. Focus on the vision of the flame. Allow yourself to be mesmerized by the motion of the flame. As you gaze at it let your vision go blurry. Soon the shift of consciousness will occur.

Water is the last element. To get in touch with this element set a chair up in front of a sink. Turn on the tap. Focus on the sight and sound of the running water. Let yourself be carried to another level of consciousness by maintaining this focus. Or run a large basin of warm water. Cup your hands and pour handfuls of the water back into the basin. Continue doing so for however long it takes for this repetitive motion carry you into trance.

You see it's not that difficult to work the use of the elements into your practice. As ever give yourself a chance to succeed with these techniques. If it doesn't work the first time, try again. Also experiment with using these techniques both in the light and in the dark. Both will bring about different results.

Simple yet effective. That's the power of the elements in a nutshell. Try your hand at them and I think you'll be pleased with the results.

Picking up the clues

I hope you've been practicing Contemporary Seidr for a period of time. You're building your Esoteric muscles so you can continue to do good work. This is great! It's a way for you to show yourself just exactly what you're capable of. But there is something I'd like to mention at this point. As you go along doing your Contemporary Seidr work you may start having clues dropped in your path.

These clues are sometimes subtle and sometimes as obvious as a brick to the head. They may sneak up on you or they may stand right in front of you blocking your path. Clues are funny things. They appear as we will apparently best respond to them.

"Clues to what?" you may ask. Clues to further growth. Clues for further exploration. Clues to important but sometimes easy to miss opportunities for your path.

The question to ask yourself is simply what to do with the clues. Act. Sometimes this work requires action be taken. It's great to drift happily around the Nine Realms. But you need to take what you encounter back with you to Midgard and learn to use it. A huge personal revelation in trance does you no good is it's not put to use.

Train yourself to be on the lookout for these clues. Had a session in which you saw a vision of a stream? Follow that stream and see where it leads. Had a vision of a sigil in trance? Write it in your journal and do some research to find out what it means.

Picking up the clues may seem obvious. But I'm often surprised when I'll be talking with a trained and experienced Contemporary Seidr worker about a trace session they've had, and they'll mention something seemingly small. I'll ask them if they've explored that clue. And they say no! Sometimes it just doesn't occur at first glance to have any meaning. That's why we need to be on the lookout for them. Something small may indeed turn out to be something big!

Clues such as this pop up. It's our job to follow them and find out what they mean. It's fascinating to do this work. The multiverse will reveal itself to you like a flower slowly blooming. Make sure to smell the flower it presents! And hunt for clues. This work should mean no less.

Contemporary Seidr and personal transformation

This is an exercise based on a trance session I had recently. It was a powerful Contemporary Seidr session and gave me much to think about. So, I used the session to come up with this particular exercise.

Go into your working trance. As an intention you are once again to travel to Niflheim. Once there allow yourself as you always do when visiting a Realm to grow accustomed to the environment. Be especially on the watch for frost giants.

A bit about frost giants. One way to view them is as your own personal baser instincts. The aspects of yourself that are less than evolved. There is nothing evil or bad per se about these aspects. But I feel we all can agree that we don't necessarily want those aspects of Self to be at the forefront. They are still raw undeveloped parts of Self that need time and space to grow. What we're about to do is give your own frost giants a space and some time to grow up at their own speed without being the face you wear to the world.

Once you're firmly settled in Niflheim stand and look to the horizon. There you will most likely see frost giants. Make yourself known to them. Yell. Scream. Wave your arms. Anything to get their attention. Once they've noticed you, they will start toward you. Now's the time to take action.

Why draw attention to yourself in this manner? The point is you want to face them so you can overcome them. This will add value to the exercise. If you face the baser aspects of yourself head on you can accomplish more spiritually.

Reground yourself. Yes, you can ground while in trance. And you're going to need it! Pull energy up from the ground until it fills your body. Once you feel the tingling of energy throughout your body hold your hands out in front of you. Point your hands palm out towards the frost giants. Allow the energy to flow through your feet up your legs and out your hands. Use the energy to create a wall of energy. A barrier between you and the frost giants. If any of the giants remain on your side of the barrier, simply use the energy from the earth guided by your hands to lift them up and over the wall to the other side. Now reinforce the barrier with more energy. And you're done and can calmly come out of your trance.

What if you find yourself arriving in Niflheim already surrounded by frost giants? What to do? Remember they are slow moving entities. It's unlikely they will do you damage before you get a chance to erect the wall. But if things get a bit hairy you can always make a quick exit. Then try coming back at another time.

There. You've just removed some of your less refined aspects of character and given then a place where they can evolve in their own time safely. You needn't worry about them popping up unexpectedly. You can face the world with greater confidence.

This example demonstrates not only the potential power of Contemporary Seidr to bring about personal transformation but also how you can take a session and build upon it. This is true mastery of Contemporary Seidr.

Allow yourself the chance to dig deeper than a single session can often allow. This is the magic of Contemporary Seidr at work.

Back to basics

You've been doing Contemporary Seidr work for a while now. You have a routine that works for you. You do pretty much the same thing every time you want to journey. Now it's time to start all over again.

Really? Why? Because all of us with time get a little sloppy. Going back to the beginning assures that you check in on skills that are fundamental to Contemporary Seidr work.

Reread the beginning of this book. Ground yourself fully every time you work? Great. Breath in a rhythm to get yourself into trance? Terrific. Use scent or drumming or other tools each time? Good. Now really examine your practices. See if there's any part of the process that you skimp on. That's why rereading the beginning of this book is helpful. It may remind you of things you'd forgotten. Hey, we're all human. We forget. And end up getting ourselves into routines that may not be the most beneficial for our work.

I go back to the beginning every several months. I know I get lazy. It helps me to review my practices in a harsh way to make sure I'm doing my best. That's all part of what makes me a successful Contemporary Seidr worker. I examine myself regularly. And make adjustments where needed.

I have an apprentice who's doing this very thing right now. He's been studying with me for two years and decided on his own that it was time for him to get back to basics. I agreed with great enthusiasm. We've done this several times throughout our studies together. I was just so pleased he recognized in himself the need to do this very simple task again. Yeah appreciate!

So, try starting all over again. I think in the long run you'll be glad you did.

Contemporary Seidr and the arts

Contemporary Seidr has many real-world applications to be explored. Take ordinary house chores for example. Doing the dishes by hand can provide the kind of repetitive motion that can easily lead to a shift in consciousness. Same with vacuuming the floor. But what of the application to Fine Arts? Can Contemporary Seidr be used for those as well? Absolutely!

I asked some of my friends who are Contemporary Seidr workers as well as artists how this works for them.

Vitki Doug Presley who is an author as well as a musician tells of riding the songs produced by his bass guitar into trance. The sound he produces as well as the rhythmic strumming strikes a perfect chord for him to sail off into trance. This way he can journey. It also gives him a framework from which he can write.

Volva, artist and needle craftswoman Saga Erickson of Stark Raven Studios reports a similar tale, but she goes into trance through the repetitive motion of sewing or drawing. These two skills give her great results in these areas. And the products she achieves are amazing! I got a ritual broom from her that is just beautiful!

She notes "Usually, I start working in either my art or my sewing first, then trance is spontaneous. As I am immersed in the act of doing, my spirit is open, and I hear and/or see. I often keep paper handy to record the words or visions. The difference in consciousness is the feeling of being in the midst of a fog that has cleared."

Artist and Volva Carrie Barcomb of Barcomb Fine Arts tells it as it is for her. "There is an ebb and flow to it — that trance brings life affirming art, heralding more poetic narrative imagery, steeped more in honest and raw messages — a combination of sense and perception connecting with undercurrents of nature and spirit. It is alive — as opposed to waking logic where it seems ego influences the rational construction of a painting, to offer a glorified impression of beauty, wherein extremes lie in the intellectual representation of the power and elitism of our material world." Her work clearly shows her connection to Spirit.

To write I often go into working trance. This leaves the creative side of my brain wide open for information to flow freely through me. If it's a topic I'm having some trouble with a working trance is often just what the doctor ordered. A cure for what ails me!

There are ways to connect into your own creativity through Contemporary Seidr. My favorite is to go into my working trance. I then connect to odr as described earlier in this book. Once I've established a connection to the orb of light that is odr I move the orb from my forehead to my navel. This area of the body in my experience is associated with creativity. I then increase the size of the orb till it fills my body. Now all I have to do is sit back and wait for the inspiration to hit!

Hopefully this gives you some inspiration on the creative force available through Contemporary Seidr. Now go write or draw or paint or weave or whatever! Get creative!

Contemporary Seidr and power areas

UPG alert! What follows is a system that was shown to me in trance by Freyja herself. The system is a nine areas of energy system that for some will resemble the concept of the chakras. It was given to me over the course of several trance sessions.

The nine different energy areas revealed to me have direct correspondences with the Nine Realms of Norse tradition. These energy areas can be used to bring about change in your life in big ways.

The nine areas are as follows:

1. The crown of the head. This area signifies Asgard. Its color is purple. It rules matters of spiritual concern.
2. Next is Ljossalfheim located at the center of the forehead. The color is dark blue, and it governs matters of the intellect.
3. The chest. Its Realm is Muspellheim. It deals with emotions and the color is yellow.
4. Svartalfheim is located at the navel. The color is red, and it deals with issues of creativity.
5. The left hand is Midgard. Brown is the color and it deals with mundane matters.
6. The right hand is Neiflheim. It concerns itself with emotions that are being held back and not expressed. The color is silver.
7. Hel is located at the base of the spine. The color is orange. And it deals with issues of the subconscious.
8. The left foot is Vanaheim. It deals with fertility. The color is dark green.
9. Last is Jotunheim. It is the right foot and deals with baser primary emotions. The color is blue green.

Great! Now what the Hel do I do with all this? This is where the fun comes in.

Suppose you are having difficulties keeping your baser emotions at bay. They are running rampant wreaking havoc with your relationships. Go to Jotunheim. The area of energy found at your right foot. Go into a working trance and see the area of energy there spinning blue green. Get in touch with that energy and color and will that the size of the area shrink. Make it smaller and smaller until it is barely the size of a pin head. And come out of your trance as always. There. You've just wrestled with the demons and won. Now you should find that your primary emotions aren't getting in the way as much. Repeat this exercise often to really address the issue. These energy areas do find ways to grow again.

Or suppose you are feeling a need for greater spiritual connection. Go into trance. Get in touch with the energy area located at the crown of your head. This is Asgard. See the area spinning purple. Now get in touch with this energy area and make the area larger and larger. Until it's as large as you can make it. And you're done. Come out of trance as usual. Again, you'll want to repeat the exercise.

Now you know one application of this system. Experiment with it. Find out other applications. Remember Contemporary Seidr work is all about trial and error. My apprentices have found other valid ways to work with this system. You can too! With this new tool in your toolbox you should have plenty to explore.

Contemporary Seidr and plants animals and rocks

Nature has a huge part to play in Contemporary Seidr. This encompasses both human nature and ecology. We have discussed a lot about human nature. Let's now take a look at ecology. Specifically plants, animals and rocks.

Plants like all living entities have a hyde or hamr of sorts. There is definitely an energy field surrounding all plant life. This is the energy we want to tap into with Contemporary Seidr.

Pick a plant. A houseplant works well. Or a tree growing outdoors. Sit or stand in front of the plant. Blur your vision until you're able to see the energy field around the plant. Note the color of the field. Notice if it's stationary or does it shimmer a bit creating a sense of movement. These are both ways the field may appear to you. Remember there are no "right" answers. Only your own experience. Remain as open as possible.

Go into your working trance. Become aware of your hyde. Find a way to reach out to the plant and its energy field with your own hyde. Once you've accomplished this meld your hyde into the hyde of the plant. Be aware of any changes to your experience. Is it hotter? More silent? As you meld your two together become aware of your vision. Slowly it should change. Slowly you'll be seeing the world through the eyes of the plant. What do you see? Shapes? Colors? Lights? Make a mental note or jot it down in your journal. You've just experienced the being of the plant. Come out of trance as usual. Thank the plant for your experience.

The same method can be used with animals. I find it easiest to do this with a domesticated animal such as a pet. But it will work with wild animals if you're quick! I find that the experience is markedly different than with a plant. The energy meld is stronger and more in-depth. Try to meld with the animal's sense of love or agape. Most domestic animals are full of love for their caregivers. It's pretty easy to ride the wave of their good feelings for us. Try and you'll see! Again, be sure to thank the animal once you're done.

Rocks can also also be connected with using this method. Although I find it to be tougher. At least for me. All rocks have a vibrational frequency they quietly emit. That's what you're going for. The sense of aliveness that accompanies each rock. I have found that crystals work best for this exercise. They tend to vibrate at a higher and stronger frequency than say granite does. But if you're patient any old rock will do. For me the sight I get with rocks is much more abstract than with plants or dogs. More geometric shapes and bright colors. This is especially true when I do this exercise with clear quartz. Wow! Some cool stuff comes up. Try it and see what you see.

Doing these exercises hopefully gets you more in touch with the ecology of our multiverse. Remember to try each exercise several times to see what results occur. Getting in touch is all part of Contemporary Seidr. Go make connections!

Working for others and ethics

There comes a time in your practice that you'll want to do this work for others. Whether a healing or a trip to Hel to talk with Great Aunt Betsy your services will be valued. This is exactly the way you want things to be. Don't be selfish with your talents. Sharing with your kin and clan are all part of the whole bag of Contemporary Seidr.

Start by working with family and friends. They are already close to you and should have some idea of what you're doing banging a drum! And they tend to be more forgiving than others if you do a session for them and come up empty handed. Sometimes we just get nothing!

When working with others it's important to really set the tone that something out of the ordinary is about to occur. The person you're working with should really get a sense that this experience is something special. So, light the candles. Burn the incense. Drum your drum. If it seems a bit like a performance, you're on the right track. Contemporary Seidr is always a show at some level. Not that what you're doing isn't deadly serious. But the more involved you can make it the better their mindset will be.

Remember that with others it's a two-way street. Ask them to help you raise energy. Have them chant with you. Try to get them involved. That way they're part of the proceedings. And besides it's a good idea to get their energy involved. Being involved makes them more invested in the task at hand. And that's a good thing.

There may come a time when you decide to take the step to charge for your services. There is nothing wrong with that. You have invested the time in study and practice. You have a skill set that others desire to take advantage of. Making this work commercial may seem to cheapen it but it actually makes the work more valuable on some levels.

Don't start charging until you are sure of your abilities. I waited two years of hard study and practice before I accepted payment for what I do. So be very sure you can bring on the goods when asked.

Reading this book and doing the exercises should not be considered enough. Only with time and experience can you attain the skills necessary for hanging out a shingle. Be sure of yourself and your abilities. Be honest. Be true to this path.

This offers a great chance to barter. Bartering is what they did back in the old days. So, it should be on the table today. I've gotten some wonderful hand-crafted items this way. Always make that option available I even had a dentist who did free services in exchange for my work!

Clients have the right to know exactly what you can and can't do. Not so good at getting in contact with the dead? Don't advertise that service. Let folks know upfront what to expect. They are paying you after all. They deserve for you to be honest and upfront.

Decide in advance what you'll do if you have a session scheduled and get absolutely nothing. It happens. We all have off days. So, decide if you'll try to reschedule for another time or just offer them a refund. But it should be clear that if you do perform the service there are no refunds. This is a somewhat touchy subject but again you must be upfront with this information.

Be clear that the services you offer are not a substitution for the services of a doctor or therapist. It is an add-on for such treatment. Never claim you can fix something. Anything. Esoteric work isn't that cut and dried. It's more a part of a process than a destination. Don't guarantee results. It's a recipe for chaos.

Use some basic common sense when approaching this. You're not going to get rich so don't allow that to be your goal. Always check in with the gods on the subject of whether or not what you're doing is ethical. Listen to their guidance.

Working for others is the pinnacle of Contemporary Seidr work. It is a powerful way to give back. And giving back is the goal of Contemporary Seidr.

Contemporary Seidr and crystals

Oh no. I know what you're thinking. "He's really gone off the deep end now." But hear me out. Crystals aren't some New Age nonsense. There are ways that they can be used effectively in Contemporary Seidr.

Crystals at the heart of things are rocks. Pretty rocks. Special rocks. But rocks nonetheless. And rocks are from the earth. What do you think all those dwarves are so busy digging up anyway? And I've already discussed rocks have vibrational frequencies. They can be tapped into and channeled just like all energy. We want to work with energy, so crystals are a perfect fit.

Crystals can have several uses in Contemporary Seidr work. The first and one of the easiest is as offerings to the gods and goddesses. I don't need to explain the long history of offerings in Norse tradition. Crystals make great offering items. Do some experimentation to find out what works. In my experience Hella responds to obsidian. Freyja loves amber. For Odin I find lapis lazuli does the trick. Loki likes carnelian. And so on. Leave a crystal on your altar to a god after loading it with your own energy. Or bury it in the ground. I make crystals a mainstay on my altar. Looks good and works wonders!

Crystals make for powerful tools in grounding and centering. Feeling a bit spacey and air headed? Meditate on a crystal. Feel the slow solid energy of the stone to help you find your balance. Any crystal works for this purpose. They are all from the earth after all!

One simple application is as a tool to help meditate. Or go into trance. Rocks have a much lower energy frequency than we do. Tuning into this slower energy until yours matches it is a terrific way to go into trance. Any crystal should do the trick. I personally match a particular crystal to the realm I'm journeying to. For

Asgard I use amethyst. For Hel I use obsidian. Part of the fun is finding out what works for you.

Another use is in conjunction with the nine power areas I've already discussed. Using a crystal of the same colors of the power areas gives the proceedings an extra boost of energy. For example, if you're working to increase your creativity use a red jasper or ruby or other red stone to help you focus on the red energy of the navel area you're working with. Tap into the energy of the crystal to send your intention out into the multiverse on that.

Crystals have an ancient history of working their wonders. Hopefully these quick examples have made you a convert. Get a few crystals to try out. Work with them. See if you can use them. If not at least they're pretty!

Utisetta

Utisetta is the ancient practice of "sitting out" to gain wisdom and insight. It is a solitary event. It goes like this.

Choose a night when you'll be able to be outdoors for several hours. Go to a secluded area and bring a blanket to place on the ground to sit on. Get into a comfortable position and sit. Just sit. Empty your mind. Perhaps go into a working trance. The goal is to allow yourself to be open to the multiverse for messages from the other Realms. The messages could come in any form. Visions. Auditory impressions. Emotional responses. Allow it all to flow over and through you. Most importantly let yourself be.

Do this for as long as you're able. An hour. All night till the sun comes out. However long you are capable of being alone with yourself in total darkness. Bring a light to turn on when you're finished and your journal and something to write with. Record the messages you've received during your time in the dark. Hopefully the images and impressions will be solid and strong. But even the faintest whispers can become profound in the dark.

Some things to prepare for before your utisetta. Choose your location for the event beforehand. It should be a place where absolute dark can occur. And where silence can surround you. The point is for the location to be as removed from the everyday world as possible.

Get creative in your choice of location. A hilltop. A corn field. A graveyard. A forest glen. All make excellent locations for a utisetta.

Go to your chosen location right before sundown. The act of watching the sun set will help alter your consciousness. Being slowly submerged in darkness has a power of its own.

Try to refrain from food the day of your utisetta. And drink only water. This will help keep your channels clear and receptive. Try also to spend the day in silence. Refrain from talking or listening to music or watching TV. Keep your phone off. All of this will help you set the mood. Ask those in your family to respect your choice of silence for the day. Explain to them what you're doing and why. Loved ones can be very supportive in this endeavor.

Urban living presents some challenges for utisetta. It's difficult to find an outdoor location free from traffic and lamp posts. So, do it indoors! The same principles apply as doing it outdoors. Select a room in your apartment or condo that affords total darkness. Unplug the phone. Remove as many distractions as possible. And have at it!

Utisetta can be a powerful experience. The messages you receive can be quite profound. The key is to remain open and receptive. Enjoy your time in the dark and silence! May you receive many messages.

Contemporary Seidr and agape

Agape is love. Not romantic love which is eros. But agape is more akin to a sense of brotherly love. It's a type of love that is expressed in love of clan, love of kin and love of the land. A very important type of love on the Norse path.

Here's an exercise to spread agape throughout the multiverse. Go into your working trance. Make this a big Contemporary Seidr session. Pull out all the stops. Incense. Drumming. Swaying. The whole nine yards. Your intention for this session is something along the lines of "I will be in touch with agape".

Get in touch with your hyde. Feel its energy. Really ground yourself and get a good flow of energy from the earth. See the color of your hyde. Now comes the tricky part. Get in touch with universal agape. Find it within yourself. For me it lives in the center of my chest. Expand that energy. Fill your hyde with it. You may experience it as a pink or green color. Leave yourself open to however it presents itself.

Once you have built up a large amount of agape into your hyde focus now of sending it out into the multiverse. This will be a dispersing type of energy form that you will be performing. Focus on sending waves of agape energy out into the multiverse from your hyde. See the waves of love like you would experience the ocean. Wave after wave of agape flowing from your hyde out into the multiverse. First you fill your hyde with the agape. Then you send out the wave. Next, the wave covers your kin. Then your clan. Then the entire multiverse. Wave after wave. Now, sense the waves flowing back to you. Back and forth. Never ending. A true give and take of this universal energy. Feel its power and might within you.

This is a correct and proper use of the power you've been learning. This is one of the best uses of your talents as a

Contemporary Seidr worker. This hopefully feels like "This is my work. This is my calling."

Don't take this exercise lightly. This perhaps is the biggest exercise I'll discuss in this book. Our multiverse needs healing. It is our duty as Contemporary Seidr workers to do our part in making healing occur. Not only on the personal level. But also on the universal level. Allow yourself to do this great work and only then will great things occur. Be part of the solution. Be great.

Contemporary Seidr in the 21st century

Traditional Seidr was great for our ancestors. It provided them answers to burning questions. It offered a form of "entertainment" in the days before TV. It had a definite place in the environment it thrived in.

But what about today? How can Contemporary Seidr be a benefit to us in the days of internet and cell phones and instant gratification? It all has to do with healing. Contemporary Seidr work is all about healing. Healing yourself so you can be able to heal your world. Heal the environment. Heal relationships. Heal those you love.

If I had to sum up Contemporary Seidr in one word I guess that word would have to be "healing". Healing on a global scale. Healing like has never occurred in modern history. And healing starts with you.

We need Contemporary Seidr today more than ever. Our planet is going through a shift in consciousness. A shift from a totally materialistic point of view to a more holistic and inclusive one. Contemporary Seidr workers are needed more than ever to help in the transition this shift is leading us to. We either take up the challenge to change or we continue on the current path which I believe will lead to destruction. Our species stands on the brink of a great moment. Where you fit in to the change is entirely up to you. You can join the growing number of people practicing Contemporary Seidr to help in the process of healing a very damaged world.

Everything I've talked about in this book is on healing of some sort. Healing yourself is the first step in joining the ranks of Contemporary Seidr workers. Contemporary Seidr is how you become more fully you. And the more you expand yourself the more you'll be able to touch others. And the people you touch will touch more people. It is a wonderful and powerful rippling effect of change. I would like to think you're reading this book because you want change. And change can and will occur. How quickly depends on us. If we all just focus a bit more on healing and less on mundane affairs like having more of everything imagine the world, we'll create! I have imagined that world. And it is why I have made this pledge to be a healer. Join me in this journey to a better world. Walk this path with me. Let's heal the world. The healing starts with you.

Conclusion

Not really a conclusion. More an invitation to study more and practice more and grow more. Your journey has just begun and hopefully will never end. Contemporary Seidr is a life long discipline and practice. My hope with this book was to give you some ideas upon which I hope you'll expand. If this book has provided you with a taste for much more it was successful.

Journeying is just the tip of the iceberg. As you travel you can gain wisdom and understanding into yourself and your personal multiverse. Beyond that there is the wisdom to be learned about the multiverse outside yourself. Discover the aspects of the multiverse you like and those you don't like. Change the things you don't like in your Contemporary Seidr sessions. Enhance the things you to which you feel attuned. The only real boundary to what can be attempted and achieved is the boundary of your imagination. Fly. As far and as long as you dare.

Happy journeying. Safe travels. And for the god's sake never stop growing!

Author list

No one lives in a vacuum. Certainly not me anyway! The books that I have read and studied over the years have all had a hand in making me the Contemporary Seidr worker I am today. Here's a brief list of the authors who have shaped my practice.

Jenny Blain

Theodoric Dukka

Jan Fries

Katie Gerrard

Kveldulf Gunderson

Runic John

Raven Kaldera

Ivy Mulligan

Diana Paxson

Evelyn Rysdyk

Try one. Try them all! Your practice of Contemporary Seidr is sure to grow.

Printed in Great Britain
by Amazon